Ultimate Guide to
Wilderness Living

Also by John and Geri McPherson

Primitive Wilderness Skills, Applied & Advanced
"How-to" Build This Log Cabin for $3,000

ULTIMATE GUIDE TO WILDERNESS LIVING

Surviving with Nothing But Your Bare Hands and What You Find in the Woods

by John and Geri McPherson

Foreword by Cody Lundin

Ulysses Press

Dedicated to those who give of their time and all too often their health and lives to ensure that we, and those like us, are able to pursue our dreams in freedom—the men and women of the U.S. Military. More specifically we single out the men that I, John, served with in the 173rd Airborne Brigade (Sep) in the Republic of South Vietnam (A Company, 1/503rd Airborne Infantry) and the men of the Special Operations Community who accomplish so much for so little.

Published in the United States by
  Ulysses Press
  P.O. Box 3440
  Berkeley, CA 94703
  www.ulyssespress.com

ISBN10: 1-56975-650-3
ISBN13: 978-1-56975-650-8
Library of Congress Control Number 2007907767

Printed in Canada by Transcontinental Printing

10 9 8 7 6 5 4 3 2

Acquisitions: Nick Denton-Brown
Copy Editor: Mark Woodworth
Editorial/Production: Claire Chun, Lauren Harrison, Judith Metzener,
      Abigail Reser, Steven Zah Schwartz
Design/Production: what!design @ whatweb.com
Cover Design: Double R Design
Cover Photographs: John McPherson
Index: Sayre Van Young

Distributed by Publishers Group West

PLEASE NOTE
This book has been written and published strictly for informational purposes, and in no way should be used as a substitute for actual instruction with qualified professionals. The authors and publisher are providing you with information in this work so that you can have the knowledge and can choose, at your own risk, to act on that knowledge. The authors and publisher also urge all readers to be aware of their health status, to consult local fish and game laws, and to consult health care and outdoor professionals before engaging in any potentially hazardous activity. Any use of the information in this book is made on the reader's good judgment. The author and publisher assume no liability for personal injury, property damage, consequential damage or loss, however caused, from using the information in this book.

Chapters

Foreword

It was 1989 and I was a punk kid attending a major primitive living skills conference. Toting a smelly deer hide, I walked up to him and asked his opinion about softening the skin based upon advice I'd just been given by another instructor. It was my first brain-tanned deer hide and I wanted it to be perfect. After listening to me ramble on, he looked at me quizzically, cocked his head, and said, "Son, we don't really care how it 'looks'—we want it to *work*."

This was my first encounter with John McPherson, and his words of simplicity and practicality have rung through my head ever since.

Years later, the world's interest in relearning indigenous living and survival skills has grown by leaps and bounds. Whether it's a new magazine article, book, or TV show, more and more people are exploring the art of primitive living skills and self-reliance. Yet, as in any other "craze," many who have dubious credibility in what they preach are eager to feed upon the body of this growing interest. Legions of media producers and editors who have zero experience in survival skills give their two cents' worth about what it means to "survive in the bush." Many of these productions not only are ridiculous in their format, but are filled with errors that, if taken literally by a starry-eyed and naïve public, may very well cause their demise.

Little by little, the simple, commonsense survival skills that kept every race alive upon the planet were being sensationalized in order to sell one more book or gain one more viewer. Commonsense reality had turned 180 degrees into a shameless bureaucracy of company-sponsored deception that honored how a survival skill "looked" rather than whether it "worked."

In similar fashion, on the educational front line, well-intentioned professors lectured students about how indigenous peoples lived, even though the vast majority of these professors had never even camped in the wilderness—let alone created fire with sticks, a canteen from a gourd, or a sleeping mat made from cattail.

Over time, the repetition of survival assumptions, half-truths, or outright lies became an all-too-trusting public's "truth" about outdoor survival and primitive living skills. The majority of the public didn't care (and still don't). A plethora of survival books, as well, have been written by authors who are not survival instructors; and, judging by their works, they haven't bothered to try out the supposed lifesaving skills they regurgitate upon the page. Even more common are survival skills practitioners who, while proficient in many physical skills, don't psychologically live what they teach. This "walk-the-talk" concept goes much deeper than simply doing a hand drill every other morning while living in the city. It is an all-encompassing life attitude that affects every decision one makes in their quest to do more with less. All indigenous living skills revolved around people becoming more self-reliant within their environment. The quest for the all-important calorie ruled the day, and there was no time or consciousness for complicated, flashy skills that didn't put meat in the pot. In essence, truly living a self-reliant life (whether the lifestyle incorporates literal "stone-age" skills or not) demands a lifestyle commitment on all levels that few can stomach.

I can count on one hand the number of survival instructors I know whose passion for survival skills includes living a self-reliant lifestyle. On this hand are John and Geri McPherson. They practice what they preach—psychologically and physically—and have done so for a very long time. The *Ultimate Guide to Wilderness Living* is a pioneer in the field of no-bullshit primitive living skills and is loaded with practical, time-tested tips, tricks, and photos that manifest only from many years of "doing it." True to John's advice given to me nearly two decades ago, this book is written in a style and spirit that embodies primitive living skills that really *work*.

Cody Lundin

Cody Lundin is founder and director of the Aboriginal Living Skills School and author of the best-selling books *98.6 Degrees: The Art of Keeping Your Ass Alive!* and *When All Hell Breaks Loose: Stuff You Need to Survive When Disaster Strikes.*

Introduction

This is not written as a survival book—it's a compilation of most of the basic skills that original peoples around the world used in their daily pursuit of life, known as "primitive living skills." Knowledge of such skills will allow you to live in the wilderness with nothing except for whatever nature at hand has to offer. In essence, the skills presented here are the ultimate in self-sufficiency. Being capable of heading into the wilderness with absolutely nothing and making a life there, not simply surviving, is the very definition of survival knowledge. So, I guess this is in some manner a survival book.

Today, everything around us—all goods manufactured by humans, whether it's the concrete we drive on, the vehicles we're driving, many foods that we're eating and the utensils that we eat them with, the computer I'm writing this on, even the paper that you're reading it on and the ink it's printed with—*everything* comes from the Earth! In our case we ("we" being mankind today) have modified parts of the Earth to create other things, manmade things. Precious few of the components of everyday "things" around us (Ford pickups, space shuttles, bread wrappers, clothing, and so on) contain elements from the Earth that are unmodified. Everything that we're familiar with has come from the Earth but has been modified and tinkered with by so many hands that it's impossible for us to see any semblance with the Earth itself. Ask most anyone to gather materials from the Earth and make the simplest of necessities, then watch 'em squirm. Primitive man, by contrast, took *everything* that he used in his daily living directly from the materials that nature provided.

Not only will this book show you how primitive peoples accomplished this, but here you'll learn, step by step, how you too can accomplish that. The purpose of this book is not to entertain; there's more than enough media out there to do that. Rather, it was written to teach you, the reader, how to actually do the skills addressed.

Several things set this book apart from other in-depth ones on the market:

- We, Geri and I, have done the skills we write about. We've done them a lot. So we write only what we've personally experienced. And it does work! If you want to know how to do it, read about it here—and you will know.

- Each chapter was first written as a complete book of its own. It was written on one or two particular subjects or skills for the purpose of teaching another person—you—how to do it. Often a publisher will dictate a list of subjects for an author to write on (whether or not the author is familiar with it), and you the reader end up with a lot of theories and wild ideas instead of facts. Here *we* decided what you need to know.

- These skills don't follow any one culture or peoples. The idea is for you to be able to understand what makes a skill work, which will enable you to travel anyplace on the planet where resources are available and for you to use that skill effectively. The rules that we developed for ourselves are to be able to take from nature only, using nothing modified by mankind.

- This book covers primitive wilderness living skills only. You'll find nothing that is superfluous. Information on edible and medicinal plants, camouflage, tracking, spirituality, and art must be found elsewhere.

There's no big secret to mastering any of this. It's all just basic physics. Once it's learned, you'll say, "Well, hell yes—why didn't *I* think of that!" Some of it (no, much of it) is time-consuming, especially in this day of instant everything. But I'm finding that many, many people are pretty sick and tired of all the hustle. This consumer-oriented industrialized society that we belong to has made most of its inhabitants dependent on others for even the simplest of needs. These skills, once learned, because of their simplicity, will be with you from now on till forever—and that's a mighty long time, folks. They need not be applied or practiced every day to stay fresh in your mind. And the comfort that comes from just knowing them will give you the freedom to know that you'll be self-sufficient to the extreme.

You gotta walk before you run, though. Understand where you're headed, and be aware that that path can—and likely will—change as you proceed. Pick one or two of the skills in this book that interest you the most, then try to gain an understanding of how and why they work. The learning and practice of most primitive skills can be done in your backyard, garage, basement, or even living room (depending on the tolerance of your wife or husband or partner). You can become proficient in them without ever venturing beyond these bounds. And if you should find yourself in a primitive situation, either by choice or by chance, though you'll find that the application isn't as easy as when done in your own backyard, you'll also find that through repeated practice you've developed the understanding and "feel" of the basic functions, the muscle memory as well as the confidence that you "know" how to apply the various methods. You'll own that special feeling of freedom that comes from knowing that you need depend on no other man, woman, or beast.

Learn the wilderness under controlled conditions. Use a tent, modern sleeping gear, backpacks, and fire making. Hike and camp in familiar surroundings where getting lost or in trouble isn't a part of the equation. Get out there in all the elements—not just when the sun shines. Learn what it's like to protect yourself in the rain and snow, especially when you're wet and cold. Add primitive things a bit at a time. Remember, though, that it would be rare to impossible for you to be placed in the outdoors with absolutely nothing, unless you do it voluntarily. Certain of the skills we detail in this book are necessary for survival: fire, cordage, traps, tools, shelter, and containers. These six skills are the basis for any living or survival situation. Everything else will grow from these.

We've read, within the past coupla years, of a group that spent some time in the wilds of northwest Montana. They had "primitive" down to a T. All their clothing, bedclothes, and gear were primitive, whether brain tan or otherwise. Primitive bows. Primitive pots. Plenty of primitive containers. Primitive fire-making sets. They had primitive under control. But, when they placed themselves "out there" in the wilderness, it appears to me that they found they lacked much of a grasp of the wilderness part. Although they commented that mice or other rodents were around and in their campsite, they never did catch any for food. In 18 days, the only food harvested by the group was reported to be one fingerling fish. When it rained they moved from their shelter to the protection of boughs of trees in their attempt to stay dry and comfortable. Oops? Maybe, but the experience will have enlightened them to this fact—a part of the learning curve. I'd bet that, next time, they encounter fewer problems.

As you read this book, you'll notice some references in the form of a thank-you scattered here and there, but no list of references. This is because, for the most part, we have learned the skills we present through a lot of fieldwork and trial and error. We, meaning all of us human beings, are the result of everything that we've encountered before. For sure, Geri and I have read or heard somewhere that to make fire by friction we need, for example, two pieces of wood to rub together. Yet it was through our own personal efforts and labor that we've learned the little steps involved to make that effort result in a fire on a somewhat regular basis. No one to credit here except us.

We learned early on that, in our day (the 1950s through the 1970s), there was no easy way for us to master skills like this. Most books on the subject only glossed over the information that we were looking for—there was absolutely nothing available that we could find to teach us "How To." True, there were a coupla books that tried to cover many of the skills described here, but we soon discovered that their authors had a lot of talk but little walk behind them. Some depended on the knowledge of others (the perpetuation of myths) and since they, the authors and editors, knew nothing about this, they had no idea that what they were passing along was for the most part garbage. It might make for good reading but failed miserably as field manuals. The reason that I early on depended on the use of a great many photographs to illustrate techniques was to reinforce to you, my readers, that we've actually done these skills, in the manner that we're presenting them to you. They do work! (Other authors can draw anything.)

The primitive lifestyle isn't for everyone—in fact, it's for very few. But the knowledge of the skills needed to live this lifestyle is within reach of anyone.

Enjoy your experience, wherever your path may lead.

John and Geri McPherson
Randolph, Kansas
January 2008

Chapter 1

Primitive Fire and Cordage

The learning of the necessary "skills" to live directly with nature, eliminating the need of intermediaries, isn't really all that difficult. You learn a little about this aspect…a bit about that one…and then another. Pretty soon you find that most of them overlap and the further you get along in your natural education, the easier it is to learn.

Many years ago when I first got serious about putting all this together (my first step was to get rid of the TV, and then electricity), I felt that if I were to learn a few of the basic primitive "survival" skills, I'd really become quite the woodsman. I soon found that the more that I learned, *the more I still had to learn.* I read (and I urge anyone interested in learning to also read) everything that I could lay my hands on that deals with living *with* nature. There's a lot written on all aspects of it—some poor, some superb, but most lying somewhere in the middle.

Before you can decide what's workable, you'll have to get out and work with it. Reading only goes so far. When you actually begin to put into practice what you're reading, then it becomes obvious just who knows what he or she is writing about.

No special talent is needed here—only the ability to follow a bunch of natural rules (physics). Any of the primitive skills, today as well as yesterday, can be carried to the extreme and become an art. I'm far from being expert in woodsmanship. I have, though, taught myself what I need to know to go "naked into the wilderness" and not only survive but before long be living fairly comfortably (unless, of course, I froze to death first). I refer to my teachings as primitive "living" skills, not "survival" skills, though they can be used in that concept. I have taught myself to be proficient in these skills—not to be an artist.

Since 1987 I've made thousands of fires with the bow and drill and with the hand-drill methods. So I'm proficient enough in this to teach it to others. The same holds true with the making of cordage. The more you learn, the more you realize what there is to learn—but the easier it becomes to learn it.

Bow Drill and Hand Drill

The basic principle of making fire with either a bow or a hand drill is really very simple. The amount of practice needed to develop that special touch which enables you to regularly succeed in this is another thing entirely.

To say "make fire" with the bow or hand drill is really a misnomer. Actually, what's accomplished is that the wooden drill spinning on another piece of wood creates friction, which creates dust, and eventually things get hot enough that a spark is created. The compressed pile of dust that has been formed becomes like the hot tip of a cigarette that's placed into a pile of tinder and coaxed into a flame.

Simple? Yeh, really it is. I've had students "make fire" within minutes of being exposed to this procedure, *and* understand just what they were doing.

I'll first show you how to make fire (bow drill first, and hand drill a little later). I'll quickly describe the necessary components and the steps to follow. Then we'll get down to brass tacks and go through it again, dwelling a bit more on how to assemble the parts and to put it all together. When you finish with this, you'll be able to make fire.

We have five components: (1) the bow, a limber stick about 30" long; (2) the drill and (3) the fireboard, both of which are softwoods; (4) a cup, called a "bearing block," in which the upper end of the drill is placed to keep it from drilling through the palm of your hand; and finally (5) the bowstring, which will be covered in greater detail later in this book.

Simplified Directions for Making a Bow Drill

We take a knife and cut a notch and a slight depression into the fireboard, twist the drill into the string of the bow, place one end of the drill into the depression of the fireboard, place the bearing block on top of the drill, and spin the drill by pushing the bow back and forth till a spark is formed. We finish by dropping the spark into a prepared "bird's nest" of tinder and gently blowing it into flame. Easy?…sure. And you might be able to make it work with no more information than this. Some 13 years ago, three of us spent the better part of a day wearing ourselves out with no more information than what you've just read—and eventually made fire.

The day most of these photos were shot, the Fahrenheit temperature was in the 40s and it was misting. I threw up the crude shelter using only what one would normally have: two light jackets and a shirt, using also rocks and grass. The purpose of the shelter was just to block the wind and rain from preventing my making of fire.

Parts of a Bow Drill

Now I'll go into more detail about all the parts—the whats and the whys, how to gather the parts, and how to fashion them under primitive conditions. The special touch you'll have to develop yourself through practice (it *does* come pretty easily).

BOW—This is the easiest part to obtain. A reasonably limber stick (limb or piece of brush), 1/2" to 3/4" thick, approximately 30" long. It needs to be limber enough to create just the right amount of tension on the string when the drill's inserted. Too limber and you'll have trouble with the string slipping on the drill. Too stiff and too much stress will be placed on the string and the drill, resulting in the drill's continually flying out on you, and most often the string's breaking. (Believe me, the stress created on the string and the drill is nothing compared to the stress that'll be building in you at

Raw squirrel skin cord "made fire" the first time. The hair rubbed off while in use; spark was found beneath pile of hair. Note thinness where skin's about to break. Fortunately, I got the spark first (note coal) and also had plenty of extra length to reuse the skin after drying.

this point!) The length of about 30" is also important, though a bow of only a few inches, or even one of several feet, would work, just not as well. At that length the bow isn't too cumbersome and will allow *for a good, full sweep of the entire length.* This is critically important, as every time the bow stops to change directions, everything cools off a tiny bit, thus impeding your efforts.

DRILL—We now need to be a bit more particular. A *softwood* is necessary. Also, dead and dry (I'll mention damp wood later). Literally dozens of woods will work for a drill. Cottonwood, aspen, and yucca are my favorites, not only because they work well but also because they're abundant in the parts of the country where I live and travel. Willow is a favorite among many firemakers. I've heard that sage works well too, as do box elder and hackberry. The smaller limbs and sapwood of cedar, locust, and ash would be fine (though the heartwoods of these are too hard). The list goes on. I've been told and have read to avoid resinous woods, such as pine. Cedar works, at least in some parts of the country. Experiment with what's available to you. Members of the cottonwood family (including birch, aspen, and poplar) can be found in most parts of the country; all of them work superbly. Search out dead limbs, preferably off the ground (to eliminate absorption of ground moisture) and with bark weathered away. Check the condition of the wood by pressing it with your thumbnail. If it makes a slight indentation easily without crumbling, it should be about right. Also, if it

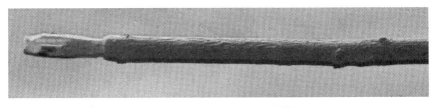

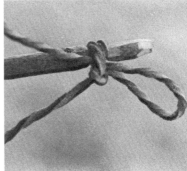

Left: One end of the bow I tie permanently, usually with a slip knot.
Right: The other end I tie with a single slip that can be untied easily and retightened as the string stretches. This is the end that I hold. This way, I can also hold any long loose end to prevent it from flying around and possibly knocking my dust pile all to hell.

breaks easily and cleanly with a snap, it has no greenness or moisture left in it. The drill needs to be about as small around as your little finger up to as big as your thumb. No real exactness here, though I wouldn't go much for larger or smaller (since a smaller drill spins more with each pass of the bow, thereby creating friction faster but also drilling through the fireboard faster, sometimes before the spark has formed).

The ideal length of the drill is 6" to 8". Too long and it's hard to manage, too short and your bow hand gets in the way of the drill and you can't see what is happening. And straight, since if there's a warp in the drill, it'll wobble as it spins and create problems. Most times a slightly curved drill can be straightened with your knife.

A fresh drill (here, yucca; my favorite combination is a yucca drill on a cottonwood fireboard). The right side is more pointed for the bearing block. The slight tit on the left helps it to stay where it belongs in the fireboard till the hole's enlarged.

FIREBOARD—The fireboard can, but need not, be the same material as the drill. Usually, it will be. Again, it must be a softwood. Check its condition, which should be the same as for the drill. The size of the board is variable. It need only be larger in width than the diameter of the drill. I like to make mine from 1 1/2" to 2" wide (remember that nothing here is exact). Take the limb of your choosing and split it in half, using your knife. Shave the split side till the board will lie flat, shave down the round side till the board is about 1/2" thick, and then square up the sides.

BEARING BLOCK—This is a very simple piece, and an important one, but one not all that easy to come up with in a survival situation. For at-home work, I suggest a 1 oz. shot glass, which fits the hand comfortably, has a hole of the right size for the drill, and has a surface as smooth as you'll find (with the goal of eliminating friction). You can also find a semisoft rock and drill a 1/2" to 3/4" hole in it about 1/2" deep, then lubricate it up with Crisco ("bear grease in a can"). You need to eliminate the friction at this end. (I have in the past used various knots of hardwoods. Some of them, though, had soft spots in them and I was coming up with smoke from my palm before the fireboard!) I carry with and use at home, in demonstrations, and in base camps a rock about 3" x 2 1/2" x 1 1/2" thick with a dandy hole in it, though it's pretty hefty to carry around in the timber. For now, this is all you need to know. We'll go into obtaining this under primitive conditions a bit later.

Since there's a definite satisfaction in taking your first ever-spark created with the bow drill and blowing it into flame, let's have you gather up and prepare some *tinder* at this time. Let's make up a batch. I really like the dry inner bark of cedar (cottonwood is good, also), plus some dry, fine grasses. Roll these around in your hands till it's fine as a cotton ball. You won't need much; a small handful will be plenty. Form a hole in it like a bird's nest. Place this on a piece of bark or cardboard (so that when it bursts into flame you won't barbecue your hand).

Using Your Bow Drill

With the information contained thus far, you're ready to "make fire." We'll run you through it once now. The information presented below is certainly useful (or I wouldn't have gone to the trouble to write it), but it deals mostly with gathering the materials under primitive conditions.

BOW—Archers, string your bow! Almost any cordage will work, but it should be strong and not too thin, as it will tend to break easily with the first-timer. Also, the heavier cordage (not rope) seems to get more of a grip on the drill. Here I'd suggest using a "rawhide" (not genuine rawhide) boot lace, which is about ideal. I twist mine tight, which seems to grab the drill that much better. In short order, you'll begin to feel precisely the right amount of tension. The string will stretch considerably with use, especially at first, and adjustments will have to be made as you go along. The bow is not strung tight; considerable slack is left. When the drill is placed in the bow, the slack is taken up (note top photo on page 9). Remember, the tension must be just so; too tight is worse than only a little slack, but there isn't much room for variables here.

DRILL—Now let's take our selected piece for the drill. I like to point the upper end a bit (the end that goes into the bearing block). When breaking in a new hole in the fireboard (as in this case), I find it easier to operate if I carve the working end into a slight "tit" (study photos on page 9). Doing this gives it a tendency to take a bit longer to mate the drill to the hole, but also assists in keeping the drill from kicking out of the fireboard while the depression enlarges to fit the drill. By the time the two mate, the hole and the drill fit better.

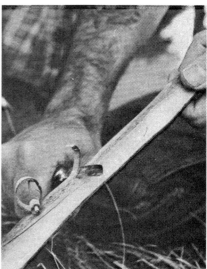

Left: Splitting the fireboard.
Right: Flattening and squaring the edges.

Cedar bark stripped from dead tree.

Shredded between fingers (or rolled between palms) to loosen and separate fibers.

Left: Bird's nest of cedar.
Right: Same of grasses.

Bow (in this case a piece of dogwood) strung with deer rawhide. I always string the drill the same way, resulting in the top of the drill being up and the drill ending up on the outside of the string, thereby staying out of the way of the bow hand.

Left: Stick selected for drill. I chose the straight middle portion.

Right, top: Scoring around the stick first makes it easier to break (**middle**) where you want it to.

Bottom: "Straightening" the drill by shaving it.

FIREBOARD—Now take hold of the piece prepared for this. There are two approaches to take here. I'll talk you through one and mention the other. Both work.

With your knife, cut a "V" notch approximately 1/4" to 5/16" wide extending into the board *almost half the diameter of the drill* (see photo below). At the point of the "V" of this notch, dig out a slight depression for the end of the drill to fit into. (The other method is to dig your depression first and then, *after* the hole has been started with the drill, to cut the notch.) The depression *must* be in far enough so that when the hole is started, the notch retains enough material at the wide part of the "V" (at the edge of the board) to prevent the drill from kicking out. If the drill does kick out, breaking off this retainer (which helps to hold the drill), you may as well begin a new hole, as if you don't you'll encounter only frustration.

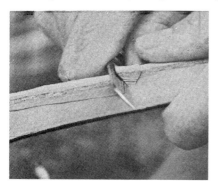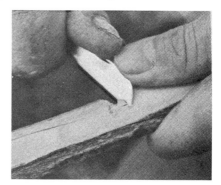

Left: Cutting the notch. **Right:** Cutting the depression for the drill.

Notches almost halfway to center of drill hole.

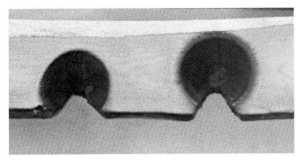

Hole on the left is too close to the edge, so the drill will only fly out. When this happens, it's best to start another. The hole on the right is great. "V" could even be a bit deeper, but this worked well.

Now, let's get serious. Place a piece of bark (you nonprimitives can use cardboard) under the notch cut in the fireboard. This serves two purposes: (1) to catch the dust and spark, enabling you to drop it into the tinder, and (2) to act as insulation between the fireboard or dust and the ground, which may be damp, cool, or both, slowing down or preventing spark creation.

The following instructions are for a right-hander; you southpaws, just reverse the procedure. Get down on your right knee (see photo next page). Place the ball of your left foot on the fireboard, making certain that it's secure and doesn't rock. An unsteady board can result in the knocking of your dust pile all to hell. I like the notch to be about 2 1/2" to 3" out from the inside of my foot, which is where my hand automatically falls into place *directly* over the notch when my wrist is locked against my left calf. Wrap the drill in the string (as noted in photo) and place the proper end into the depression of the fireboard. Take the bearing block in your left hand, place it on top of the drill, and lock your left wrist *securely* against your left calf (this is important, as you want the hand holding the bearing block to be completely steady; if it sways to and fro while drilling, you'll be inviting trouble). All that's necessary now is to run the bow back and forth. At this point you'll start developing the "feel" of what you're doing.

The amount of downward pressure applied to the drill, *combined* with the speed of the bow, is what determines how much friction is created, thus how quickly a spark is formed. When you first begin, don't even think "fire"—instead, concentrate only on becoming comfortable with the operation (kinda like chewing tobacco and walking at the same time). Make smooth, full strokes with the bow, running it the entire length of the string. Remember that every time you change directions, that split-second stop cools things off just a little. Keep the drill perpendicular.

The string has a tendency to wander either up or down the drill while spinning. Control this by pointing the end of the bow either slightly up or down, whichever seems to work. *The pressure that you're able to apply with your thumb and fingers of the bow hand on the string will also help.*

*Before you begin to "make fire," have all ingredients at hand. **From left:** fireboard, drill, bearing block, strung bow, tinder, four piles of kindling in various sizes, and, at **far right,** larger wood—all laid out on my vest to keep them from absorbing ground moisture (the ground was wet).*

Drill straight up and down, with left wrist locked securely against left calf.

Vary the amount of pressure on the drill. Begin with only a slight amount and increase it as you become more comfortable. Too much pressure, and things will want to bind up and the string to begin slipping on the drill. Whenever this happens, you *must* let up on your pressure, because no matter how fast the bow's moving, if the drill isn't spinning there's no friction. If not enough pressure is applied, nothing will happen.

When beginning to mate a new drill to a new hole (what we're doing here), there'll be a certain amount of drilling where nothing seems to be happening. This can last from only several seconds to several minutes, depending on the type and the condition of the wood. At first the drill will spin smoothly, as if sliding on a freshly waxed floor. Then suddenly, as the drill and fireboard begin to "mate," it will act as if you've gone from the waxed floor to sandpaper. This difference you feel, and hear.

Now, control and feel become all-important. The drill, which to this point was easy to control, suddenly becomes more difficult. You may find that you need to slightly tilt the wrist holding the bearing block ever so slightly one way and then the other as you run the bow back and forth, so as to keep the drill from kicking out of the hole.

Right after the two mate, and the first smoke and dust appear, I usually take a quick break before I go after the spark. This allows me to catch my breath and relax my muscles so that when I start up again I'm fresh. This often makes things a bit easier.

At this point, bear in mind that the hole isn't yet deep enough to hold the drill on its own. It still will take some care on your part to keep it from kicking out. Now that the friction has begun, the drill is slightly more difficult to control. You'll feel this, in short order. Vary the amount of downward pressure on the drill to coincide with the speed of the bow. *You will develop the feel.*

Here's another *very* important tip. I had made fire this way for 11 years before stumbling onto this technique, and now I can't imagine ever having made fire successfully, regularly, without having applied it. As mentioned before, the string will stretch while in use. A good, flexible bow will compensate for a lot of this, but eventually the string will become so loose that it slips on the drill when you apply the proper amount of pressure. Once, just as the spark was about ready, my string began slipping badly. Without thinking, I took the string between the first two fingers and the thumb of the bow hand and took up enough slack so that I was able to successfully finish. Now, anytime I take up the bow, the fingers and thumb just naturally wrap on the string (see photo below).

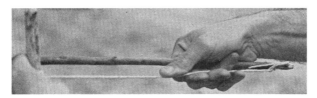

Note how I use my thumb and fingers to control string tension. Use whatever's most comfortable for you.

If you concentrate on keeping the drill perpendicular—the left wrist locked tightly against the left calf, the bow taking long, smooth strokes, the fireboard steady and not wobbling—the spark will form of itself. First the smoke will begin, then dust will rise, then heavier smoke, and the dust will get blacker. Keep yourself relaxed and merely concentrate on the smoothness of the operation. There *will* be a spark.

Once the drill and hole mate, the spark will normally be created in less than 30 seconds. Once, timing myself, I had a spark in 10 seconds. If everything is working, it doesn't take long.

When you have your spark (most of the time it'll be hidden—the dust pile's smoking is your sign), carefully lift away the drill and place it aside. There's no big rush. I've left the smoldering dust for up to four minutes while I went in search of tinder, and still had a fine coal. Pick up the bark or cardboard holding the spark, fan it some with your hand, blow gently on it, let any slight breeze help (*not* a wind strong enough to blow it away, though). When it glows, drop it into your bird's nest of tinder. Fold the tinder over the top and begin blowing the spark more and more as it gets hotter. Suddenly...fire!

Left: Note black dust and smoke—a spark is there. **Right:** Dropping it into the "bird's nest" of tinder.

Left: *Blowing tinder to flame.* **Right:** *Adding the first of the finest shavings of kindling.*

Left: *Adding larger kindling and (***right***) adding larger pieces of wood. On wet days, the inside of most woods will be dry. From spark to good solid fire (as in this series of photos) took less than a minute, but to get the spark took longer than usual because of wet weather and gusty winds.*

When I first began making fire this way, I had the tendency to wear myself out by the time that the spark was formed. Someone else had to blow it into flame because I would just blow the whole damn thing away. No need for this. If you concentrate *only* on the control of the drill and the smooth operation of the bow, taking extra care to remind yourself to remain calm and relaxed, the spark will form on its own and you'll be left fresh enough to easily blow the spark to flame. If you're getting winded, you're doing something wrong.

Many times it seems that no matter what you do, a spark simply won't come into being. The chances of this happening seem to rise proportionately with the size of the crowd that you're demonstrating this to. But *when*—not *if*—you do get that spark, whether it's the first or the hundredth, cherish and glow with it. It's something that I never take for granted. Like calling coyotes, there are so many things that can go wrong, yet each time it works I feel a real sense of accomplishment.

Some Observations on Using the Bow Drill

For the last few passes of the bow, some folks advise that you apply slightly less pressure on the drill, to kick out the spark that may be under it. I usually don't find this necessary, but if unsure of the spark I sometimes do it.

If I seem to have difficulty getting a sure spark, I often make several furious passes with the bow at the last. I don't like to do this, though, because it has the tendency to wind me. Then I lose control of the operation at this point and the drill kicks out, knocking away the dust pile.

Usually you can tell that the spark has formed, because you'll see a wisp of smoke rising from the dust, separate from the smoke created by the drill.

On occasion, the entire pile of dust will suddenly glow—a good sign!

A single hole in the fireboard is capable of many sparks. Before using it again, it helps to slightly roughen the tip of the drill and the hole.

After several uses, especially with too tight a string, the drill will become too "round," causing the string to slip. This is usually easily corrected by carefully shaving it till it's once again unround.

Ear wax, or oil from your hair or the side of your nose, will help to eliminate friction in the bearing block. Always remember that you're eliminating friction at the bearing block, and creating it at the fireboard.

Avoid placing the wrong end of the drill into the fireboard, as that little bit of oil can really foul things up.

Under damp conditions, find and use the driest woods available, and get into the driest location that you can to work. If the wood's only damp, it can still work, but it will take a lot longer. The spinning drill eventually will dry things enough to work, though you'll have a lot of strikes against you.

Under primitive conditions, the hardest components to gather will be the string (covered later) and the bearing block. Sometimes you'll find a ready-made block in a stone with precisely the right depression, but don't count on it. You might find a piece of bone that will work (say, from the skulls of small critters). Also look for a piece of hardwood, possibly containing a knot with a slight hole that you can easily enlarge. If you find something that might work, you can form or enlarge the hole by using the bow or drill. Use a *hard* piece of wood for the drill (or maybe you'll be lucky enough to come up with a "natural" rock drill), definitely something harder than the block material. Ingenuity and common sense help a lot.

Hand Drill

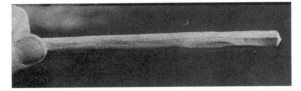

Top: *Note how cordage has "rounded" the drill.* **Bottom:** *The drill has been shaved "unround" and a tip formed for starting a new hole.*

To now explain to you how to make fire with the hand drill will be simple—at least in theory. In practice, though, you'll be faced with a much greater challenge than the bow or drill. The basic principle remains the same: to create friction with a wooden drill on a fireboard. The spinning of the drill, the fireboard, the notch, the dust, and the spark—all seem somewhat the same. But...

Parts of a Hand Drill

DRILL—The material for use here differs little from what we covered for the bow drill, except that because of the extra difficulty in creating friction here you need to be more choosy. The ideal length of a hand drill, for my length arms, is about 18" to 24". I usually begin with a few inches longer, as this shortens quickly. Too long a drill and the top has a tendency to whip around, causing you to lose control (so much more important here). Too short, and you don't get the full benefit of a long downward run of the hands before having to return to the top once again. I prefer a diameter of about 1/4", to gain more revolutions of the drill for each sweep of the hands (a drill that's too thin and limber will bend from the hands' downward pressure).

 FIREBOARD—Again, the basic type is the same as for the bow or drill. I'd been having trouble catching a spark, when someone suggested a fireboard thinner than the one I'd been using. When I cut down the cottonwood board that I had been using to about 1/4" to 3/8", things improved. With the softer yucca, I still keep the board about 1/2" thick. With the hand drill, I begin the depression and hole *before* I cut the notch. I also cut the notch slightly different than for the bow drill. I keep it closed at the top, flaring it open toward the bottom of the fireboard (note photos on page 20). I find that the drill has cut the hole below this point before things get hot enough to matter, and that the closed top then forces more of the *hot* dust into the notch, rather than letting it spill over the top.

Note that the last 1 1/2" of this cattail hand drill was slightly shaved, to remove some but not all of the outer shell.

Using Your Hand Drill

To put this in action, get into a comfortable position. My left foot again holds the fireboard, but your position may not be the same. For me, it's slightly different. I need to place the foot out a bit further and drop my knee out of the way somewhat, so that I can get a good *full* run of my hands down the length of the drill. I use the side of my heel to hold the board. Your hands must come down *straight.* You *must* keep the drill perpendicular. By placing my foot and knee slightly different than for the bow drill, I'm able to start my hands "rubbing" at the highest comfortable point (in my case, 24") and to keep them going to a point about 6" above the fireboard. Once you reach the lowest point, raise your hands again to the top *one at a time,* so that you can keep *constant downward pressure* on the drill. If any air is allowed to reach under the drill, it cools everything off. Once both hands are up, repeat the procedure. Eventually the smoke, dust, and spark will appear—though not all that easily.

This procedure will wear you out, I assure you. A completely new set of muscles is at work here. After you've done this for 45 seconds or so, you'll feel as if you've run the Boston Marathon, yet using your arms instead of your legs. It's strenuous and it takes a lot of practice to get this operation down *smoothly,* which it must be to be successful. I suggest that you do a lot of practicing before you even think "fire." This is a bit more complicated than chewing tobacco while walking. Here you must also juggle. It does take practice, not only to get everything running smoothly, but also to get yourself into some semblance of physical well-being. This does sap your energies. (Anyhow, it does mine.) It also creates blisters on the palm of your hands, which eventually will turn to calluses if worked at long enough. It took me well over a month of daily workouts to develop a good set of calluses, which a four-week vacation of "city living" took away.

Some Observations on Using the Hand Drill

When you first attempt making fire with a hand drill, I suggest going slow. Get the movements down to where everything runs smoothly and automatically. Your hands clasp the drill at the top, you rub the drill between your palms (keeping *constant* downward pressure), you keep the drill perpendicular at all times, when your hands reach the bottom you grasp the drill with the left hand's thumb and forefinger, you raise the right hand to the top and hold the drill firmly while the left hand comes back up (thanks, Bob!), then repeat...repeat...and repeat. Over and over, slowly at first, and then speed up as it becomes more natural to you. Speed and downward pressure are all-important.

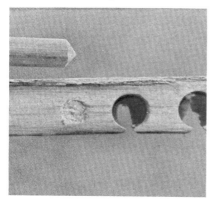

Left: *Fresh cattail hand drill tip and depression in fireboard.*
Right: *The hole is begun. Note carefully how notch is cut. A cattail drill and a yucca fireboard are easy for the hand drill.*

Spitting on your hands helps retain a little extra "grip" on the drill (thanks, Bryan!), allowing a few more spins before your hands reach bottom. Always put the thickest end of the drill down, as this kinda slows the hands' trip downward also.

My most commonly used drills are stems of cattail or mullein (thanks, Dick!). Most of these stalks are just slightly bent, though. They must be straight, so be selective. I know of one woodsman who uses only willow. Since an ideal drill is sometimes difficult to find, a good idea is to make your drill beforehand out of whatever wood you like (I prefer the dogwood that I use for arrowshafts), then splice a tip of your choice for the working end (see photos opposite).

I find that the outer shell at the base of the cattail is just enough tougher than the inner portion that it tends to wear faster at the outer edges, leaving a hole that looks like an anthill. It won't work this way. To compensate for this, most times I'll find it necessary to slightly shave the outside. This takes practice to remove precisely the right amount. Further up the stem, I don't find this problem.

Left: Hand drill spliced to receive a softer tip (here yucca). Below: Splice wrapped with sinew, showing how to hide loose ends. Just pull the right-hand string and the noose will pull tight.
Bottom: Spliced tip ready for service.

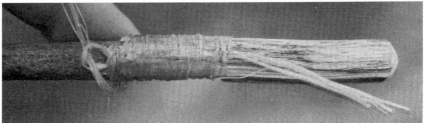

This is difficult for me to explain, and probably more difficult for many of you to understand, but before my first sparks arrived with the hand drill (they still don't come with regularity) *my mind and body became "one" with the drill and fireboard!* You may or may not experience the same, but this has happened in all cases when I've successfully gotten a spark with the hand drill.

By using a longer drill and superb *teamwork, two people can make this easier by keeping the drill spinning constantly. It takes two working in harmony—one set of hands picking up the drilling at the top precisely when the other set leaves off at the bottom.*

Another two-person variation that I've come up with (I haven't heard or seen this anywhere else), this is by far the easiest of the hand drill methods that I've worked. Use a bearing block and have one person apply the downward pressure. The other spins the drill vigorously, instructing the "bearer" how much pressure to apply. The spinner, not having to apply the downward pressure, isn't exhausted so easily, enabling the spark to be quickly made.

Cordage

To me, any description of the use of the bow/drill that doesn't include the making of cordage is incomplete. Such a common thing as a piece of string just isn't always in your pockets when you may be in need of fire, especially in a survival situation. And when you most need this fire (in winter cold and damp), you don't really want to tear your clothing up to make a string. Even if you did, you may not know enough about how to prepare it to keep it from breaking under the stress you'd place on it when using the bow and drill.

Top: Hemp cordage still attached to the unprepared strip. ***Above:*** Stinging nettle cordage. This piece "made fire" with the bow and drill.

This section will teach you how to make usable cordage of the kind that's able to withstand the use of the bow and drill. I've personally used the cordage types that I state are suitable for this. I'll also mention by name others that I've heard or read about but not tested myself. Some readers of this book are likely to have with them certain valuable items (handkerchief, dog fur, human hair) in the most primitive situation, and may find others commonly afield. For additional sources, once you've soaked up the information contained herein, you can experiment, letting your imagination be your limit.

 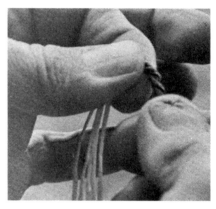

Upper left: Black and white strands hanging from fingers. *Upper right:* Twisting the blacks tight clockwise for about 1/2" and then *(lower left)* twisting that counterclockwise over the whites and twisting the whites clockwise. By continuing this simple process you end up with cordage *(lower right)*.

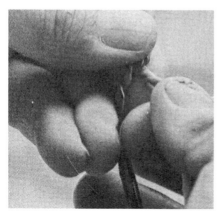 

Making Cordage

I'll attempt to describe this simple craft by words—something not so simply done. I'll also use photos of my own, since I'm more adept at taking them than at arranging words.

Let's begin. Take several strands of thread; any kind or size will work. Let's just make them 3' long for this demonstration. Lay them out on a flat surface and use a magic marker (or anything similar) and dye the strands black or dark for one third of their length (that's 1', folks). You don't have to dye them; the color is added simply to make the process more understandable on this trial run. Pick this bunch of strands up *at the point where the dye begins*. Now, you have hanging from your fingers two lengths of strands, one being 2' long and white, the other 1' long and black. Correct? You right-handers hold them between the thumb and forefinger of your left hand. Let's say that the shorter black strands are now the ones uppermost in your grip. Begin with these (my reference to these individual strands will now be references to either the black or the white—still with me?). Now, take these black strands and *twist them tightly clockwise* (that's to your right) for 1/2" or so. Twist the now-twisted black strands *counterclockwise*, over the yet-untwisted whites; hold them securely. Now, twist the whites *clockwise* and twist that over the blacks *counterclockwise*. You'll find yourself always working the top bundle as they switch places.

That's it—the entire secret. Just keep doing this till you're within a few inches of the end of a strand, and splice in more, to continue for as long as you like. (See photos on page 27.) Keep the splices at different intervals on the two sections, to keep the whole stronger. Constant splicing of few fibers makes for a stronger whole. The twisting *clockwise* of the individual strands and twisting them *counterclockwise* into one strand is the way to do it. The contrary twisting holds the whole damn thing together. It's a very simple concept—till one tries to put it into words.

With this knowledge, your life in the wilds takes on a new dimension. You don't have to think for very long before the possible applications start forming in your mind. From threads to ropes, the list of uses for cordage is endless.

Cordage materials need to be strong enough for the task at hand, but also *must be pliable*. Although dry grass would certainly be strong enough for the bow or drill (as well as numerous other uses), its brittleness makes it unusable. It would break immediately just tying a knot.

We'll begin with what you're likely to have with you when thrown into a survival situation: a neckerchief or scarf, or something similar. Tear this into strips approximately 1" wide (a normal neckerchief is about 18" square). Pick up the first strip as with the fibers (in thirds) and begin the twisting action as described above. When reaching the end of one strip, I tear the last 2" into thirds (also with the new spliced-in strand) to help interlock the splice, and on I go. When I reached 3 1/2' with the kerchief I was working, I quit with 5 strips left over. (See bottom photo opposite.) The advantage to being able to use this technique is that in a survival situation you might have access to a T-shirt, or some bandages from a first aid kit. The list of possibilities goes on.

If you're lucky enough to get lost with a furry critter, so much the better. I worked with the underfur of a dog and found that I had an unlimited supply on hand. It wasn't all that difficult to get the hang of working with it, either, though different than the longer fibers I'm more accustomed to. In a few hours, I ended up with a good solid rope about 3 1/2' long. When making fire with the fur, though, I found that it stretched easily and slipped badly on the drill, till I wetted it—then it worked like a charm. You might also come across the carcass of a furbearer (coon, coyote, and the like) where enough leftover fur might be lying around. (See photos on page 28.)

Something that most people will have with them is a supply of hair. If things got tight, you could cut your own. This works well. I ended up with a good strong rope in little time (not my own—donated by Margie's Country Image). The hair that I worked with was about 6" to 8" long, though a bit shorter would also work. Again, it's easier to work with if wetted first.

Plants for Cordage

The list of fibrous plants that can be used for cordage is long. I won't cover them all, as I don't know them all. I've never worked with dogbane (also called Indian hemp), which I've heard is about the best plant around.

Stinging nettle, velvetleaf, and hemp (marijuana) are three similar, widely distributed, and common plants (weeds?). All make a good, strong cordage easily capable of withstanding the stress of the bow and drill. Using dried plants, I take a rounded rock and lightly pound them to break the stalk, and then tear this into strips (roughly thirds). I then begin at the top of the plant, "break" the inner material, and then "strip" the outer layer loose.

Additional fibers ready to splice in.

Halfway spliced.

The finished splice.

Cordage from neckerchief strips.

I follow down the plant, breaking and stripping about every inch (this works better than just stripping the outer fibers, which will tear easily). (See photos opposite.) I end with a rough strip, maybe 2 1/2' to 3' long. This I gently roll between my fingers or my palms to separate the fibers and to remove the chaff. What I end up with is suitable for cording.

Left: Dog fur. **Right:** Human hair.

The leaf of the yucca gives a strong fiber that's also easy to work. It can be used either green or dried. With the yucca leaf, the fibers are inside. Take the dried leaf and beat it gently to separate the fibers some. This helps it to soften faster while soaking. Then soak the pounded leaves till supple. When your yucca is partly or fully green, take a rounded knife blade (flint or otherwise) and scrape the outer covering from both sides (the soaking makes this easier with dried leaves). Then work the fibers loose by rubbing back and forth with your fingers. Superb cordage material.

Gently pounding the stalk.

Pulling the stalk of dogbane apart.

Breaking the inner stalk and stripping it from the fibers.

You can come up with additional usable fibers with only a little experimenting. When in the timber or fields, just grab different weeds and grasses as you go along, break them, and try to separate the fibers. If they hang together in strips, try using them. Grass will work and can be fashioned into a great rough cordage suitable for baskets, mats, or insulating liners to winter camps.

While on the subject of plants, let's not forget tree barks. The inner barks of many are fibrous and work superbly, as with the fibrous plants. Cedar makes a fast though weak cord. Look around a bit in your area to find what's available. Not often thought of, the inner or outer *nonfibrous* barks of most trees will work well also, especially for the emergency bow or drill. What I used in my test was the inner bark of the Osage orange (I was debarking bowstaves). First removing the rough outer bark, I then carefully withdrew thin strips of the next layer. The average length I ended up with was about 3', a super-good length. I cut these down to about 1/4" widths and shaved them till about 1/16" thick. This individual strip I then used as I would a bunch of strands, twisting away. When I reached the end of a strip, I cut about 2 1/2" of the ends to splice into my many thin threads, and continued on. This made *one of the best* quickie bow or drill strings that I've worked with (besides maybe rawhide). Once dried, it wasn't worth a damn—too stiff and brittle, plus you can't cord it when dry. But when wet (green), superb! **Caution:** When using the bark from any live tree, though, do so *only* in an emergency, as it damages the tree (and could even kill it). If it's necessary to use a live tree, take individual strips of bark from several. This helps to ensure the life of the tree. It also would be better for the tree if you stripped the bark from the branches.

Scraping off the outer covering of the yucca leaf.

The spiny-tipped wild yucca plant.

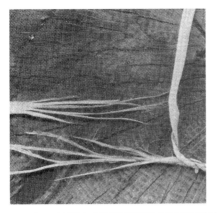

Upper left: *Solid piece of bark ready to splice.*
Upper right: *Splice halfway worked.*
Bottom: *Finished.*

Animal Material for Cordage

Now, let's discuss some animal material. Sinew (tendons) supply some of the strongest cordage available. An animal is loaded with sinew in various lengths. The longest and the easiest to work with are the long strips running down either side of the backbone (silver colored, lying on top of the meat, running from under the shoulder to the hip). Sinew is most easily removed with a dull knife, to prevent accidentally cutting it. Scrape it clean and then lay it out flat to dry. It works easiest if dried first, then broken and separated into threads of the appropriate size, and finally wetted again before cording. The resulting strong cordage was the most common of the Indian bowstrings. The shorter tendons of the legs are also usable, only not as easily since they're shorter and thicker, which makes them harder to separate and work with.

Left: *Deer rawhide cut 1/4" wide.*
Right: *After soaking, doubling, and twisting, then stretched to dry.*

Rawhide for Cordage

Rawhide is another good cordage material. It's best used after it's dried, primarily because drying eliminates stretching (note that I'm still talking string for the bow or drill!). With rawhide, I don't actually "cord" it. Instead, I double it and twist it up fairly tight, stretching it and tying it off at both ends to dry. I find that the doubling, twisting, and stretching eliminate the stretching while in use (I use this for bowstrings); add strength; and also help the rawhide to grip the drill better. I cut the deer rawhide 1/4" wide, a width that seems to be plenty strong enough. I've shot up to several dozen arrows through 55- to 60-pound bows that I've made, and have yet to have one rawhide string break.

I once took a squirrel skin and cut it in a circular strip about 1/2" wide, leaving the hair on (as if under a primitive situation). Then I twisted it tight, but not doubling it, and made fire with it the very first time. (I had trouble keeping it tied to the bow, because with

*Wild weeds: (**left**) velvetleaf and (**right**) hemp.*

the hair on and the skin green, the knots didn't want to work all that well.) The string, as would any green or wet rawhide, stretched badly and took *much* finger control to keep taking up the slack. Also, after the first fire, I was unable to use the same drill till after it had dried. The moisture from the skin got the drill so wet that it did nothing but slip. Once it was dried again, though, I had no trouble.

But enough about cordage. You've now got sufficient information to go out, identify certain usable plants and other materials, work with them, and put them to your use. You also have learned enough to be able to search out and experiment, to come up with many more. This is not an exact science. Just bear in mind the important rules of length and pliability of the material used.

A Coupla Fire-Making Tips

Kennie Sherron of Ponca City, Oklahoma, sent me the following two fire-making ideas. They will add greatly to the methods explained in this chapter.

*A fire drill, as Kennie describes it, for the Indian who has it all. Made from deer leg bone, it's squarish and will never "round." The bone being hollow, it's reinforced at both ends to prevent splitting (here with rawhide). The piece shown **above at left** is permanent, to fit into the bearing block. The lower piece, pulled out here, is a replaceable soft tip. When I first got this in the mail, I just kinda put it aside, but carried it along for show-and-tell. Well, at one set of demos we actually ran out of usable drills near the end of the second day, after more than a hundred-plus fires. But we did have some short pieces of yucca, and so gave this a try. I knew that it would work but was unprepared for how well it worked. The squarish bone spins like a champ in the bow, and the extra weight of the overall drill gave me much better control. And, most importantly, we now had enough fire drill tips for several hundred more fires. I like it!*

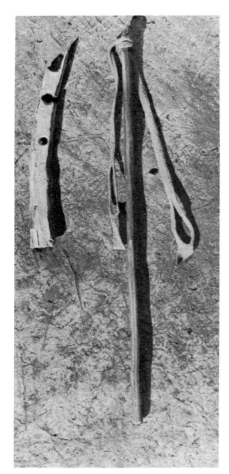
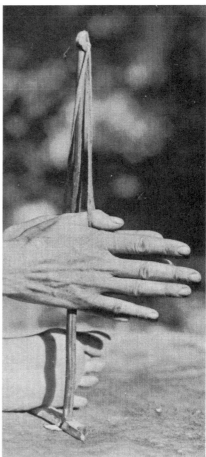

Another, probably more important, tip for a fire-maker lacking a helper: this one for the hand drill, whose use, even under the best circumstances, is never easy. It's a piece of cordage (or, as illustrated here, a strip of brain-tanned buckskin) with slits cut for the thumbs, tied to the upper end of the drill (and also tied over it, in most cases). The thumbs placed in the slits provide constant downward pressure, letting you constantly spin the drill. Makes starting a fire almost easy, and greatly increased my successes.

Chapter 2

Primitive Tools — Making and Using Them

For the most part, in this book we will be using modern tools to show you how to maintain life in a survival or wilderness situation. But, you might ask, "What's the purpose of learning a complete series of *primitive* wilderness living skills if I have to resort to modern technology to accomplish them?"

Great question. We feel that the best way is to learn the skills themselves, then learn how to do them the *hard* way, this time using primitive tools and implements.

Hard way? As you'll see in this chapter, "hard" is the wrong term. "Different" is a better word. Different and more time-consuming. But in adapting primitive to our modern lifestyles, aren't we trying to get away a little from the time-consuming, overly complicated, highly mechanized, and artificially powered tasks of ordinary life?

Of course, you can read up on any of these subjects in a variety of reference books, and watch all kinds of demonstrations that you may find on the Internet. But if you don't just jump right in there and apply yourself, nothing's gonna happen.

Learning to make and use primitive tools in a day-to-day situation really isn't hard. Still, we feel that if you're trying to learn to master tool making while at the same time changing your accepted approach to using such tools, you'll be spending a lot of extra time and encountering much frustration. Therefore, we teach the skills first, and then we teach how to accomplish them with primitive tools. As you'll see, eventually it all naturally ties together.

But what do we mean by "tools"? Our *hands* are tools, aren't they? I suppose that, for our definition, here we'll be making tools for our hands to use to do the projects that we'll be covering. That will pretty much encompass any project that you're likely to happen upon in a primitive situation. There are three important points about tools:

- ❧ Tools need to be made from materials that can be found in nature: *stone, shell, bone, antler, horn, wood,* and so forth.

- ❧ Just what do we need these tools to do? *Gouge or poke, chop, pound, bash, split,* and (most important) *cut.* Put yourself in a primitive situation without a cutting implement of some sort, and you won't do very well.

- ❧ Methods of manufacture include *flintknap, peck, grind,* and *burn.*

Now I'll try to break this down into some semblance of order.

First and most importantly, you need some type of cutting tool—a pocket knife, so to speak. Think about all the projects that you do, or would like to do, or might have to do, in your daily regime in the wilds, and what tool will be the most important? A cutting tool. Let's begin with that.

Basic Flintknapping

Now, don't look at some of the photos in this chapter of fine blades and put the book down, thinking "I can never do this." You may be right, maybe you can't. But the tool that you're going to need to cut and chop your way into or out of the woods is indeed within your grasp. Read on.

A lot has been taught, and some little written, about flintknapping, which is the art of systematically turning stone, particularly flint, into functional tools. ("Knap" simply means to break with a quick blow.) *Some* of what we've seen in print is good, a little of what we've read is very good, but most is just trash. Almost nothing generally available to the student of primitive wilderness skills attends to the very basics, the most important aspect of knapping: that is, the obtaining of the spall or flake either to be used *as is* for the tool or to be *turned into* a tool. This first basic function of spalling, called making the flake, is the most important part of knapping.

Without it you can travel no further. With it, there's nothing more you need to know.

Most certainly we've had help from others in learning what knapping we know, but we've found that even the most willing of teachers weren't answering the questions that we didn't even know we needed to ask. All who knap certainly possess some grasp of what the principles are but they (1) weren't conscious of what they were doing (it just came naturally, and it worked), or (2) they didn't know how to present what they were doing, or (3) *they had advanced so far that they had forgotten the importance of the basics.*

A good many modern flintknappers have learned their skills backward, doing the last step first. I know that I did. Here we start at the beginning,

Left: *Fancy blades, yes. But in our actual primitive workings they account for probably less than 5 percent of the actual workload.* **Right:** *These easily made flakes do the majority.*

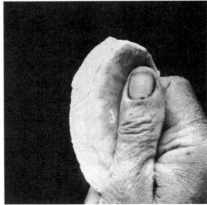

The functional, simple, easy-to-learn, easy-to-make, one-blow tool.

Safety

Please take care to follow these safety precautions when doing any sort of flintknapping. You have only two eyes, and one pair of lungs, and the normal set of limbs—and you'll want to protect all of them.

- *Wear eye protection when working stone*. It doesn't take but one misdirected sharp edge to eliminate sight.
- *Don't breathe the dust*. Every time that you remove a flake from the stone, you'll create dust. Once in the lungs, it cuts and creates scar tissue that will be there forever. It doesn't go away, like when you quit smoking. Those tiny razor blades do some serious cutting. And the resulting scar tissue will eventually kill you if you breathe enough of the dust over a long enough time (think "silicosis"). Be aware that the dust not only is in the air, but also gets into your clothing and whatever. Best not to do your flaking in the house but instead do it outside, letting the wind clear the air for you. Most dust masks won't work; some will help a bit (something is better than nothing).
- *You're going to cut yourself,* so keep a supply of bandages handy. If you wish, wear gloves or use a piece of leather while holding the stone you're working with. We don't do this anymore, but we occasionally still cut ourselves. Also, be cautious of where the falling flake will land. I've more than once driven a flake into my leg. Be cautious and you'll be all right.
- *Don't flintknap* (especially the advanced blades) *in the company of those with sensitive ears*. The accompanying language is similar to that of auto mechanics.

Flint

Just what *is* flint? Well, according to the dictionary, flint is a form of quartzite. The description of quartzite is a bit more complicated, so I'll simplify. I'll lump all the stone that we'll work "flint like" into one category and call it *flint*. As far as I know, there are only two sources of true flint in the United States: Georgetown flint, from Texas; and White River flint, from South Dakota. The rest are cherts, jaspers, chalcedonies, agates, and plain old quartz. To my way of thinking (here goes my theorizing again!), most all of these are just various stages of development or quality of quartzite (as coal is to diamonds). Quartzite cobbles are pretty common, nearly as close as your local streambed or road cut. Generally, the better-quality flints are smooth and have a sheen. The poorer ones are more grainy (as in sandy). Most have an outer coating, sort of like a limestone covering, called the cortex ("cortex" is the commonly used term, though "corticose" is the more proper). Cortexes vary in workability. Some can be left on and used with the tool, but others are too crumbly and won't do the job at hand. The cortex can hide the flint underneath, so you'll need to do some experimenting to find out just what's what (applying the rules that follow).

Left to right: First, cobble of Dover chert from Tennessee; light brown inside, dark brown cortex. Next, cobble of chert from flint hills of Kansas; white limestone cortex, dark blue banded ring of high-quality chert with lighter colored interior of lesser quality. Third, lens of knife river flint (chalcedony) from North Dakota, rootbeer colored and translucent; white, hard, smooth cortex.

Many of you are familiar with obsidian that's used in the making of "arrowheads" and other tools. Obsidian is also workable under the same rules that follow. It's simply natural glass made by volcanic action. Obsidian is the easiest of these materials to work, it gives the sharpest edge known to us humans, and it's great for beginners and advanced knappers alike. Its drawbacks? It's quite brittle and *extremely* dangerous (thousands of tiny dust razor blades to be breathed into your lungs or stuck into your various body parts). Many flintknappers who haven't worked obsidian kinda knock those who do work with it because of its ease of workability, *but most of those knocking it wouldn't be able to turn out a fine, thin, long blade from obsidian without breaking it first*. In this book we'll call it all "flint" and ignore the obsidian, though the principles are the same.

One quality that all these rocks possess is that they're homogeneous (of the same composition throughout). Simply put, they're all one, there's no grain to them (unlike the grain in wood), and energy will travel equally in *any* direction that it's directed.

Techniques of Working Flint

You can predictably remove flakes from a stone in three generally accepted ways. All three have similar, but different, rules:

- ❦ *Direct percussion,* where you hit the parent rock directly with another rock, an antler, or a wood billet (a short, stout piece of wood).
- ❦ *Indirect percussion,* where you place a blunt pointed tool (such as an antler tine) at the point of removal of flake from the parent rock, then strike this with a billet.
- ❦ *Pressure flaking,* when you place the antler (or wood tool) against the parent piece and remove a flake by applying pressure.

Here we'll work primarily with the basic *direct percussion* method, just touching on pressure flaking as a means of resharpening. Pressure flaking can also come in handy in platform preparation.

With direct percussion what we're doing is striking one rock with another (wood, antler, and bone are some other tools that can be used). Now, for our purposes, almost any rock will suffice as a hammerstone, even the same as the core, but this isn't recommended. The better case is to use a sand-type stone, but not some crumbly old piece. It should grip the platform (defined below) for just a microsecond to allow the energy to be released smoothly and yet be strong enough to take the abuse. The hammerstone deforms as the core bites into it. The harder the flint, the harder should be the hammerstone.

To remove large flakes from a large nodule, you'll need a large hammerstone. I prefer to work with a fist-sized *and smaller* hammerstone for my general work, as this fits comfortably in my hand and seems easier *for me*. The smaller the hammerstone, the more force necessary for flake removal; and the more force exerted, the less the accuracy. And accuracy is important. You'll discover that if the rock is properly struck, the flake will separate easily.

Rules

To make finely flaked, long, thin blades, you first must learn many, many rules and have (usually) years of experience. In order for you to make the stone tool necessary to perform the functions outlined earlier, you need to know only two rules. With them, you can be turning out tools (flakes) almost immediately. This has been argued by one of the country's foremost knappers, but I have proved him wrong many times. In fact, after one session I conducted of 45 minutes or so, 3 of the 15 students present were doing just that—and they were on average 11 years old! The rest didn't seem to care.

Two rules. Pay attention, now. Your practice will be your finished tool. Two rules (I repeat myself purposely), one more important than the other: (1) the *cone* (angle), and (2) the *platform*. The cone is the more important.

The **cone** determines how rock will break when struck. Flint breaks conchoidally. The instant that a force strikes the surface of the flint, the energy is transmitted into a *cone* radiating at about 120°. The break in the stone pretty much follows this cone. The significance of the cone is that it determines at what angle and where you must strike a blow in order to remove a particular chunk of stone.

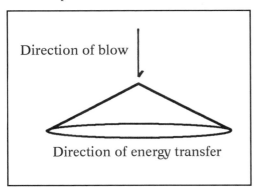

Direction of blow

Direction of energy transfer

The **platform** *is the surface that the blow is delivered to*. It must have a particular shape, or the blow will be ineffective. The platform can't be crumbly or fragile. If it is, the stone will crumble when struck, rather than fracture cleanly. The platform is the edge of the stone forming an angle of *less than 90°*. The importance of the platform is that it determines whether or not a blow will produce a flake at all. You can beat all day on an obtuse angle (more than 90°) and not produce a *predictable* flake, or you can strike a weak platform and ruin it. Note various platforms in the following text and photos.

You can know only the concept of the cone and produce tools, or you can know only the platform and not produce any. Know and be proficient with both, and you'll be a beginning flintknapper. You'll be able to remove flakes from a stone in a predictable manner. Conversely, you'll be able to predict what's left behind after your work is done. You'll be in control.

Each time you remove a flake, you need to prepare a new platform for the removal of another flake from the same area. At each stage, before a blow is struck, you need to study the rock and ask yourself what must be the angle of the blow to the core to remove a targeted flake, and then you must ensure yourself of a good, solid striking surface (platform).

The cone—the all-important cone. All knappers are well aware that it's a physical law that you can't flintknap without some knowledge of the cone. There are literally hundreds of rules that must be followed in the course of advanced flintknapping (not covered in this book), but you'll find that a good share of them are dictated because of the cone.

Remember, the line of force isn't a straight cleavage, like splitting a block of wood with an ax; rather, *it's a circular cone* (note photos). This line of force, as it were, I can't stress to you enough. Once you become aware of what it is that I'm saying, a little light in your head will flash a "Bingo!" sign and you'll find yourself with a damn good comprehension of what's happening. Like most other primitive skills, there's no magical formula—just regular laws of physics that, once understood (along with lots of practice), will enable you to be in charge.

 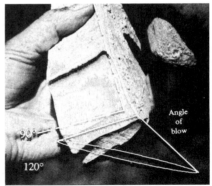

When striking a blade from a core, the natural tendency is to want to strike in line with the intended blade to be removed (**dotted line**). Due to the conchoidal fracture principle, the energy will then go too deeply into the stone; you want it to more or less "skim the surface."

Above right: Note that when the angle reaches or becomes greater than 90°, the energy runs too deeply into the stone for flake removal.

 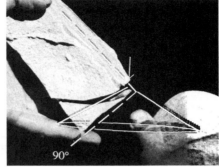

Left: Note the angle that the core is held in relation to the blow. (Most beginners tend to not compensate enough.) The correct angle is pretty severe. *Right:* Note how the flake tends to naturally curve outward from the cone and into the core. Note the surface (the platform) that's struck by the hammerstone; it's solid, with no weak overhangs.

That worked so well, let's do it again! Really, this is all-important. Notice that we're removing flakes from rounded areas or corners (there's a reason for this, which I'll explain shortly). ***Above left:*** Note once again the striking surface (the platform).

*This set of photos illustrates the removal of thin and thick blades—thin for surgical slicing, thick for scraping or chopping. Note that the angle and placement of blow are the determining factors. The angle here shows clearly. Blow placement should be closer to the edge for thin (**above**), further in for thicker (**below**).*

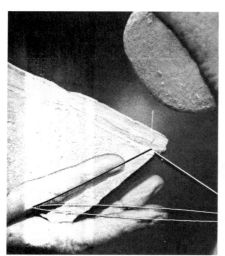

Oops! Too severe an angle.

Try again on the other corner, and get better results.

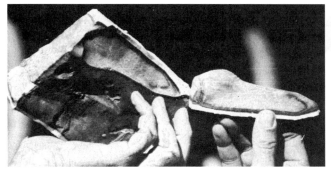

Left: A wide, long, thin blade is removed by striking nearer the edge but further "around the corner" into the straight plane and holding the core at a more extreme angle. The result: a sharp blade (right) but one that will dull easily.

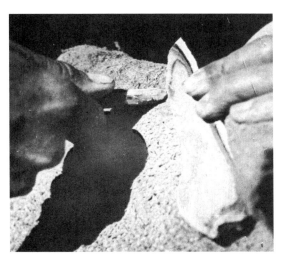

Left: The edge is resharpened by pressure flaking, here using a rounded piece of hard, dead dogwood. Pressure flaking is the final phase of flintknapping. Pressure is applied to the piece till a flake pops off in the opposite side. Here wood is used. Antler or bone make for better tools. To protect the hand, a leather pad is used. *Below:* The resulting sharpened edge.

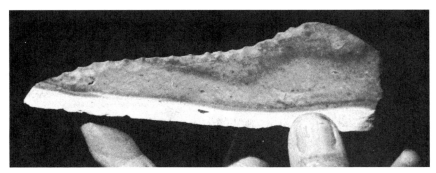

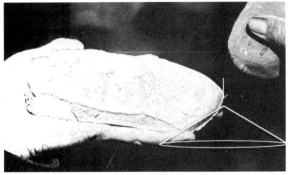

Left: *A natural lens of chert. The cortex in this instance is crumbly, so its edge is neither sharp nor durable. We remove a series of flakes (below left) to give us a better edge (below). Note that this tool is used much throughout this chapter on various projects.*

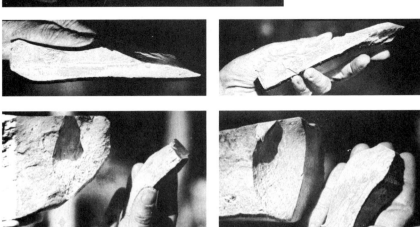

The two photos above accentuate well the cone-shaped flake. This is accomplished by striking a bit farther back on the platform and allowing the energy to flow deeper into the stone by not angling it quite so much. This gives a more solid-edged tool for scraping and chopping.

*Good examples of average, working flake tools. **Left:** "Inside" of the flakes, with the sides removed from next to the core. The lower is the end that was struck. **Right:** Side views of the same flakes, the left side being the side "struck" (platform). Note that no lines are straight. The line of force, as it travels, tends to bend outward, away from the line of initial force (cone) and into the parent rock (core).*

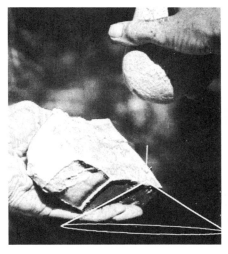

First three photos illustrate well why a corner or rounded face is necessary for predictable flake removal. The mass of the core simply holds onto the flake. The sides won't release it, though (right) you sometimes can call a usable blade from a straight edge.

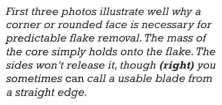

Platforms

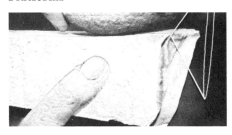

Upper right: *Unprepared platform from top and side view. Thin, weak overhang will collapse before dissipating energy properly. To clean up this weak overhang, pull your hammerstone as shown (**above**). (Big-time knappers use an abrasive grinding wheel, found at the local hardware store, for this. Use what you have available, which often will be only your hammerstone, remembering that the conchoidal principle is still at work here.)*

Above right: *Resulting prepared platform.*

Another view of platform preparation. **Top:** *Unprepared.* **Bottom:** *Ready to go.*

Top: *Weak platform.*
Bottom: *Results that you should expect.*

Support

We've established that when you strike a rock, the energy is transmitted conchoidally—into a cone. Still, there are some variances. If you were to strike a blade from an end of a long, slender piece, shock waves from the blow travel through the rock haphazardly. If the rock weren't supported properly, these haphazard shock waves may snap the piece in two at the unsupported end. So be aware of this for some of your basic work. (Note photos.)

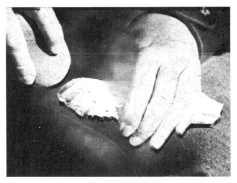

*Three common ways to support a piece. **Above:** First, here the hand's doing the supporting, though this particular piece is almost too long for free hand support. The far end is held against the palm while the fingers hold the worked end.*

***Right, top:** Second, lay the piece on your thigh (in this case without a pad, as would be the case in the field). Most knappers use a thick leather pad. In this photo the worked end alone is resting on the thigh while the other end is simply "supported" by the knapper's other hand. The entire piece could be resting on the thigh.*

***Right, bottom:** Third, in this case, the worked end is free while the other end's supported by being pushed tightly into the thigh.*

Discoidal

When working with oval, flattish quartzite cobbles, you'll sometimes find it easiest to "get into" the rock or to simply remove a blade using a method taught by Boulder Outdoor Survival School and given the coinage "discoidal." In this operation, a cobble (ideally about 6" long, 4" wide, and 2" deep) is swung onto an anvil stone (something substantially larger and harder) and strikes near the end of the cobble. This will remove a roundish sharp flake. This is the same concept that I've already discussed, only in reverse, with all angles the same. By using the space left from the flake removed as a platform, you can then remove another flake from the reverse side by conventional percussion, and then another, giving you a useful handax—one of humankind's oldest stone tools.

With the discoidal technique, the flake is removed by the same rules, only the hammerstone here is the anvil. Two tools: the flake and the core. Using the platform formed with the flake removal, a handax is readily created by simply removing more flakes (knives).

A flake knife tool (left) and a handax (below).

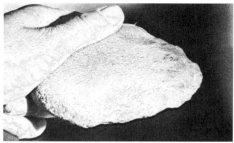

Bipolar

The term "bipolar" here doesn't mean what you think it does. When smaller cobbles similar to those described above are the only stone available, you're still not without a knife. By taking the flattest of these and placing it up-ended on an anvil rock, you can split these neatly in two by striking a blow on the top. What this does is drive the energy directly through the stone to the anvil and then back up. Some stones are definitely harder than others, so several blows may be indicated.

> **Watch those fingers—it's easy to smash them. And wear protective eye gear (or close your eyes just before you strike).**

With normal percussion flake removal, an angle of less than 90° is necessary (as noted earlier). What, then, to do if all you have are egg-shaped rocks? One answer is to simply throw one against another and hope for the best. But to do it like the "big boys," and retain some control, we can turn to bipolar here, also. My limited experience with this, using larger pieces (mostly obsidian), has shown that, despite drawings showing the contrary, an egg-shaped rock that's hit in a bipolar fashion on an anvil rock doesn't always neatly split in two. So direct your blow carefully, and ***be certain to close your eyes*** just before contact (even *with* eye protection). Pieces of sharp stone can, and will, be flying all over the place. You *will* end up with basically two halves, giving you the beginning of a core for flake removal.

Splitting a small cobble in two with bipolar can be tough on fingers but does **work.**

*Splitting large pieces in two (**above**) works better on paper than in practice (**above right**), though on occasion it does succeed (**right**).*

Some Notes

🍃 It's difficult to remove long flakes from a flat surface (because the energy is cone shaped and tends also to curve outward and into the stone).

🍃 Flakes will tend to follow ridge lines (certainly, as there's no mass on either side to prohibit the cone from releasing).

🍃 It's difficult, maybe impossible, to shoot flakes through a valley. The energy will stop at the far side of the first ridge and probably "hinge" (create an abrupt line of stoppage). It's almost as hard to run a flake through a "hill" (over 90°).

🍃 A good practice is to draw the projected flake to be removed on the stone with chalk, and then carefully study the results. This will eliminate haphazard banging (*tip from Scott Silsby*).

🍃 The ideal flake can be removed from a surface that's off a platform of less than 90° (at and above 90°, the energy is shot too deeply into the "mass" of the stone). The outer surface runs smoothly, with no abrupt "hills" or "valleys" to impede the energy flow, and the surface is somewhat rounded (as with a ball).

Recommended

Once you have the understanding of the concepts placed forth here, you might want to advance even further. The only complete book that I'm aware of that's worth its salt is *The Art of Flintknapping* by D. C. Waldorf. Its only drawback (that I know of) is that it doesn't begin with the basics—a good reason for my own book! The first time or two that I went through it, I was ready to trash it. I simply wasn't able to comprehend what it was that the author was saying. It was too advanced. But, once I got some basic understanding under my belt, I took in more and more of its principles. I still read it occasionally and each time pick up more. *Get it.*

Another primer on this subject is *Flintknapping—The Art of Making Stone Tools*, by Paul Hellweg. Online sources can help you find used copies of many useful books on the topic.

Whew!

I'm sure glad that's over with! Not that the subject of flintknapping is so difficult, as you've no doubt seen. What's difficult is finding the right words and putting them with the right photos to make it all gel.

Let's proceed now to discuss other materials we can use for tools when caught in a survival or wilderness situation.

Trying to figure some sequence for what follows has been about as time-consuming as doing it. You'll find that much of what I'm laying out from here on to the end of this chapter ties back to the basic principles of stone working (knapping). You'll also discover that working with one resource requires, on occasion, working with another. It's that old *circle* of primitive technology that kept so many of our ancient ancestors alive and kicking (thanks, Great-great-great…grandpa!).

What I've done now is kinda laid out the photos that Geri and I have created for this chapter. I'll write around them, since they speak much better than any words or drawings of mine could. Since we've been concentrating on sharp edges, let's continue along those lines.

Shell

Whether thick ones or thin ones, shells can be used in many ways as tools. Heavier ones can actually take quite a bit of abuse as choppers or scrapers, though probably the most common use would be as a cutter of some sort.

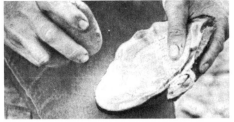

Heavier shell is here percussed with a hammerstone into a sharp, serrated edge.

*Shell here is thinner, (**upper left**) being pressure flaked to a serrated edge (**upper right and far right**). **Right:** Raw shell and other half that has simply been ground to an edge on sandstone.*

Sandstone

Various grits and harnesses of sandstone are very important tools in the production of tools.

Heavy Blunt Instruments

Simple tools such as heavy blunt instruments have lots of uses, from driving stakes to mashing nuts. Of course, the easiest way to use a tool is to simply grab the nearest rock or piece of wood and bash away. On the following pages we'll refine this quite a bit.

Wood

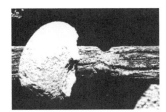

*Chopping (**left**) with handax of tough quartzite, this hard piece of Osage orange took less than 10 minutes to score deep enough to break (**right**) where we wanted it to. Finished club (**center**) has had the hand grip chopped to a size more suitable for our hands.*

Stone

Rocks can, of course, be used as is. You can also shape them to about any shape you wish, by pecking (continual hitting with a harder rock). Not difficult, just time-consuming. This illustrates the pecking of a groove into a very hard piece of rock, using an even harder piece of jasper. Holding the piece in your hand or on your leg is recommended, as the pecked rock may break in two if placed onto a hard surface. (Hafting will be illustrated further along.)

Bone and Antler

Antler and especially bone are common finds of any gatherer. All animals die and, unlike humans, their remains are allowed to renourish the Earth from whence they came. If you can come upon them before they disintegrate, these can be dandy additions to any tool kit.

Knives, projectile points, wedges, scrapers, needles, fishhooks, and awls are just a few of the many uses of these items.

The most common and easiest way to downsize bone and antler into workable sizes for most tools is simply to bash them with a blunt instrument, though this certainly isn't the most reliable method. If time and patience permit, scoring (cutting a line into the bone along which you desire the break to occur) beforehand can bend the odds in your favor as to which direction the break may happen. The deeper the score, the better. Some real fine, long awls and needles have come from leg bones that had been properly scored lengthwise. Moist heat will temporarily soften them, making scoring and cutting much easier. With antler, however, overboiling will weaken it considerably. Scraping with a stone blade and rubbing on sandstone will add the finishing touches. In fact, a piece of sandstone is often the only tool necessary to finish out a piece.

Bone

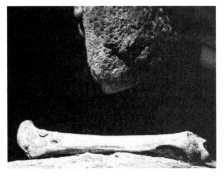

*Using a rock as our basher (**upper left**), we reduced this deer leg bone to more manageable pieces (**upper right**). Some grinding on sandstone (**lower left**) gave us a nice awl, projectile point or knife, and a fishhook (**lower right**). Simple bashing and grinding produced these tools in mere minutes.*

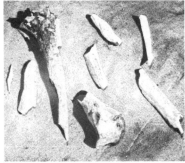

Antler

Similar to bone, in characteristics and workability, is antler. Through our own personal experiences, we've found that antler is more flexible than bone and so will take a bit more abuse. Also, it seems that the molecular structure of antler is tighter than that of bone, allowing us to get sharper cutting edges. Horn, no examples of which are shown here, seems to be even more flexible and tighter in molecular structure. (We define *antler* as the outer projection growing from the heads of certain animals such as elk and deer, and *horn* as the outer sheathing of antler on such animals as cow, buffalo, and sheep.) Shown here are several examples of things to make from antler.

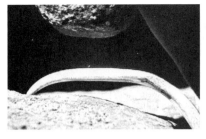

*Right top: Antler from skull cap to where we just broke it. **Middle:** Same piece after bashing off skull cap and grinding on sandstone to make billet for percussion flaking flint.*
***Bottom left:** Two small wedges or chisels.*
***Bottom right:** How it all places together.*

*Left top: Wrong way to break deer antler; tip will break off, we know not where. **Middle:** Better way. Note where gap under antler is, where it does break (**bottom**).*

*Elk antler. **Above:** About to strike with rock at score mark. **Right:** Where it broke, precisely at the score. The underside of the antler broke out of the score (this could've been corrected by scoring deeper).*

Below: What a few minutes of grinding on sandstone accomplished to turn this into a fine wedge.

Digging Stick

One of humankind's oldest tools is the digging stick—simply a pointed stick that is used for digging or prying. It, of course, requires the use of tools in making.

Which end to use...?

...and then chopping (fire also could be used as a tool to burn it to length)...

...fire hardens the end by driving out moisture and also makes it easier to point...

Result: A very functional, durable, hard-pointed digging stick.

Wooden Awl

While we're still working with wood, let's do another quickie project, again using tools to make another tool.

*Using our trusty quartzite handax and wooden maul (**left**), we split the leftover end of our digging stick (**right**).*

*Then we chop it to shape with a flint ax (**below left**), shave it further with the sharp flint, and finally (**below right**) grind it on sandstone to end with (**bottom**) a finished awl or possible needle using the natural knothole.*

Celt

In previous pages you've seen the making and using of choppers made from quartzite and flint. Here I'll show another common approach to the making of an ax—the celt (pronounced *selt*, and related to prehistoric stone or metal implements shaped like an ax head). Made from what most refer to as *greenstone* (green is its more common color in certain areas), the stone is actually a mixture of minerals (basalt, jade, and hematite are some common celt materials, though each locale has its own). It can be found almost anywhere, located often as cobbles, but also may be found in veins.

The property that we're looking for is a certain degree of hardness and smoothness so that the piece will *grind* down to a sharp edge but will also take abuse. We want a hard, dense, tough rock. Several types break conchoidally, which in many cases (such as here) helps in reduction. One test is to remove a flake, grind and polish it, and then attempt to break it with your hands. Some of these stones won't flake, in which case pecking with another, harder rock may be in order.

The celt illustrated on the next page took fully eight hours to make. We've found that knapped flint axes take minutes to make (versus hours for ground axes), and sharpen themselves as the edge chips (as opposed to weakening and dulling for the ground), thereby leaving us to maintain that the flake flint ax is economically better.

*Breaking in two (**left**) a large lens of "greenstone" by laying it at the edge of a rock and placing a well-struck (and lucky!) blow using a hammerstone. Then reducing it by percussion (**right**) to a more manageable size.*

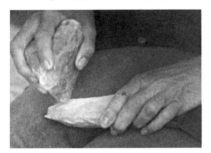

*When presented with certain high areas, pecking (**left**) can be the solution to more quickly removing material. Most time will be spent in grinding and polishing (**right**) on various surfaces of sandstone.*

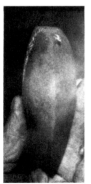

*Finished celt has (**left**) flattish top to help prevent splitting of handle, tapering toward the rear (**middle**) so as to fit into hole in handle, and a proper angle at the cutting edge (**right**). Too thin an angle will break too easily, too abrupt an angle won't cut as well.*

Hafting

The placing of an ax, celt, or other tool onto a handle can really make your work easier. It's not all that difficult to do, once you've become familiar with working with the various natural materials. Since we just made a celt, let's now haft it.

Top left: The roughed-out handle after being reduced by fire and chopping; *(right)* beginning to burn hole by placing a coal and blowing through tube; *(left)* directing the burning by blowing onto firebrand. Burning the hole can be tricky. Once the area is charred, it will ignite and burn readily. To prevent burning where you don't want it, remove the char. The hardwood won't ignite as easily. You can also place water or a slurry of clay in areas you don't want to burn. When the hole becomes deep enough, the fire starves for oxygen and you need to blow constantly. You can burn from the opposite direction after reaching halfway.

Sizing of the celt to the hole is critical. Contacts at the top and bottom must be spread evenly the entire thickness, with the surfaces laid flat to help prevent splitting out of the handle. I like to include a "Y" at the top of the handle, as I find this stronger; leave about 2" at the top. Some woods split easier than others, so it's wise to check this out before you get 4 to 6 hours invested into making the handle (this handle took 4-plus hours to make). Elm, yes—cedar, no. The weight of the wood is rather important, also, as heavier wood makes for less work when chopping. The hole is tapered, as is the celt, so that friction from use seats it tight. A gap of at least 1/16" needs to be left at the sides, otherwise the celt will spread the handle out and split it. (Special thanks here to Scott Silsby for his efforts in helping me try to explain the qualities of "greenstone," a not-so-easy task.)

*On smaller grooved hammers or axes (**two left photos**), we've wrapped the handle itself around the stone, twice on the left one and once on the right one. Most green saplings or limbs are very flexible and are made even more so by boiling or heating for a short period. They've then been held in place with natural fiber cordage, the one on the right permanently to be used as is and the one on the left to be reinforced with a light rawhide wrapping sewn on with sinew (**as in two right photos**).*

To mount a blade on a stick. you can saw into the end with a flake: the most time-consuming. Or simply split the piece in two, carve out a channel for the blade, and then bind it all together, gluing it if you have something. The easiest that we know of is this trick discovered by Larry Dean Olsen. Pay special attention to this group of photos.

Right photo group, top to bottom: (1) Blade is laid alongside shaft and notches are cut (A) leaving behind the size you want the groove to be. A thin line is cut (B) where split is to stop (depth of groove). (2) The notch is carefully split on both sides to line (B). (3) Shaft is turned and the groove is "popped" out by bending in both directions from line (B). Pay special attention to where the fingers and thumbs are placed for pressure points. If you're not careful, the shaft will simply break at its weakest point, the notches. (4) The results.

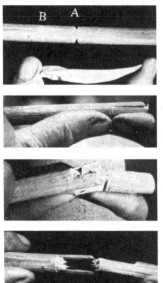

Right photo group: Once groove is made, it's best to custom fit the piece, especially stone. Remember, few straight lines with stone flakes. **Left:** *The initial fit; by trimming with a sharp blade, the piece is made to fit better (**middle**). The resulting knife or scraper (**right**), lashed into place with natural fiber cordage, may not be the strongest but will still do a number of chores. Lashing with sinew and setting the piece with pitch or hide glue would make it extremely durable.*

Adze

The adze is a specialized tool used for trimming and shaping wood. The blade itself can be made from "greenstone" and ground *or* flaked from flint, as done here. It's mounted opposite from an ax, at right angles to the handle. Unlike the ax, the blade will be flatter on one side than the other, allowing more careful removal of wood.

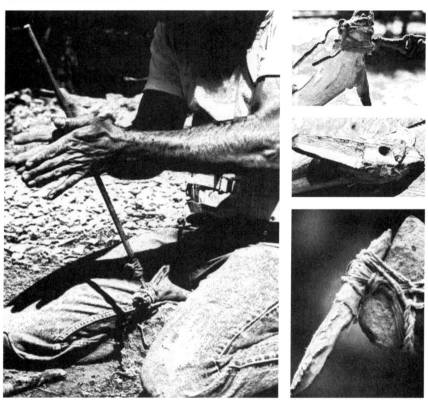

Left: *The blade sits on a solid platform of the handle, and it can break off. I'm repairing just that by having glued the separated platform back on and lashing it in place, then drilling a hole with a hand drill mounted with a stone point and plugging the hole with a carved piece of hardwood glued in place.*
Right top: *Another method of attaching the blade is to wrap it in rawhide or buckskin for cushion and tying that to a flat-ended handle. This works well by absorbing a lot of the shock.*
Right middle: *Drilled hole.*
Right bottom: *The finished repair job, and it has done a lot of work since.*

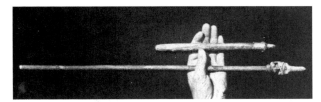

Two drills with stone tips hafted as shown on page 65, the longer a hand drill and the shorter for use with the bow drill.

Vise

We're kinda stepping up in the world now, talking about a vise, of all fancy things! Primitive peoples surely had them, in one form or another. This trick was shown to us by a flintknapper and old-time trapper from Colorado, George Stewart. The one illustrated here is on a small scale and is shown holding an arrow-shaft-sized stick, though this could all be upscaled and used for bows and the like.

...tie securely at bottom of split to keep it from opening too wide.

Drive a stake into the ground...   *...split it down about 6"...*

Make a loop of strong cordage near the top, insert a stick and twist it tight to hold whatever. Tie or otherwise secure the bottom of the leverage stick.

Working with the Tools

To this point in the chapter, we've dwelt primarily with the making of tools, though many also used some previously made ones. Now we're going to do a coupla projects that are aimed only at *using* your tools in a wilderness or survival situation.

One project that covers most primitive tool usages is the bow (detailed in full in Chapter 4), so we'll head to the timber in a bit and show you how to do this with tools we've made up till now.

When working with students we stress the importance of being capable of heading into the wilds and making a fire (Chapter 1) with nothing but what's available. This is what I'll cover first.

Preparing a Fire Board and Hand Drill

Begin with splitting the hearth...

...then gouging a depression to start the hole.

*Use a thicker blade to carve most of the notch (**top**) and a thinner one for getting into the tight area.*

Scoring drills helps to prevent their splitting, as they pop easily at the mark.

Making a *Primitive* Bow

*Once you've got the tools, you then cut
the tree down, chop it to length, and
split it.*

Cut and split...

...scrape bark off, using flake if necessary...

...cut to length...

...chop to shape, using either handax...

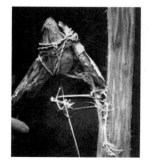

...or Adze...

...split off any excess...

...then line the bow out, here using charcoal.

*Up till now we've worked with green wood. To cure it out, we now tie it (**top**) in whatever position we desire the final bow to take. (This "quickie" bow procedure we learned from our good friend Jim Riggs of Oregon.) Let it dry from several days to more than a week, depending on the wood (the denser the wood, the longer). In this case, we let this piece of eastern red cedar (actually, a juniper) dry for one week in our hot basement. At this point (**left, middle**), the roughed-out bow is just that: rough. But with some little scraping (**left, bottom**), some careful cutting (here of the grip), and (**right**) sanding with stone, we end up with (**below**) a pretty much finished-out piece, surrounded by some of the flake tools used.*

*There are any number of positions for you to experiment working in. Here Geri buries one end of the bow (**upper left**) into her belly and the other into a secure area in a rock and draws the flake toward her to remove wood shavings in a hurry. She then (**upper right**) uses adze to make final cut to length and (**bottom left**) shapes up end with a sharp flake before (**bottom right**) cutting notches.*

Below: *The finished bow. (For more detailed instructions on the making of bows, see Chapter 4.)*

Finis

So there you have it. You'll note that, in the section on flintknapping, there was little to no mention of arrowheads or other projectile points. Well, there's a reason for this, which I hope you've picked up on by now. *They simply aren't that important in primitive living.* A sharpened stick will kill just as certainly as any "arrowhead," if properly placed. In any case, the making of projectile points is a schooling of its own, usually requiring years.

The tools that we stress as important require no more time than it took you to read this book and to have a little sit-down to apply.

With the exception of only a few items interspersed, everything shown in this chapter was made for the production of this book. The celt and handle required over 12 hours total. The bow took one afternoon to cut and prepare to tying down, and an additional better part of a day to finish out. The majority of the rest were made in one afternoon. This ain't to brag, just to reinforce to you that this really isn't all that difficult. If we can do it, anyone can.

I'll finish out this chapter by showing you a few other objects that we've made using the techniques shown in this book.

Some things often forgotten, when speaking of tools, are food preparation items. Both the mano-and-metate and the mortar-and-pestle are more than a little useful when living primitively, in terms of grinding staple items such as seeds, acorns, and corn.

Wooden Bowl

This bowl was made from a piece of aspen, following guidelines set forth in this book and using stone tools and friction-made fires. (See Chapter 8 for further details on making wooden containers.)

Mano and Metate

Geri and I made this small metate and the accompanying mano of pumice (or perhaps basalt?) for use in our small camps and demonstrations. The two items are used as a pair for grinding corn, grinding acorns into flour, and so on. The depression was created simply by grinding with the mano.

Mortar and Pestle

This mortar was made in just a few hours by pecking with the same piece of jasper shown on page 56.

Chapter 3

Primitive, Semipermanent Shelters

Some of my fondest memories are of sitting in a shelter tucked under pine trees or in a forest of oaks and other hardwoods, with the wind howling, a freezing rain or snow outside, and inside a blazing fire and a warm drink.

We've seen and heard much on shelters from other experts with outdoor backgrounds. When people learned that we were working on a book on shelters, almost to a person they urged us to include the basic shelter: the *debris* type. This is little more than a glorified pile of leaves, grass, and sticks that you can crawl into, much like a sleeping bag, to get out of the cold and wet. It insulates you from whatever you want to be insulated from. It does it well. But in this chapter we'll do little more than touch on it.

When Geri and I were kids, it was only natural to build a shelter of this type, as it didn't take much imagination or skill. Yet I can think of three instances of where this shelter comes in handy: a true survival situation when you won't have time to complete a better shelter, *including making a fire;* in a situation where the instructor doesn't want to take the time and effort to show the student better housing; and finally, where the instructor doesn't know anything more.

A debris shelter has lots of problems. If weather is bad (reason for the shelter), you're locked into your bed till it changes. If you venture out, you'll end up wet—something you don't want when you're trying to stay warm.

So in a true survival situation, you're pretty well stuck looking at leaves and grasses at nose length and lying around waiting to get found (you're also insulated from sound and well-camouflaged). If, like the vast majority of modern woodspeople, you've *placed* yourself into this woods situation, when you finally get bored, you get up and go home.

I've been accused, most of my life, of being somewhat crazy for spending so much time outdoors in rain and snow. But when I venture into the elements, I try to be comfortable. I've spent the vast majority of my life "camping out" during the winter months, both as I was growing up in the mountainous southern tier of New York State and also for the last 40-plus years in Kansas. Winters get *cold*. Some of my friends may have thought that when I ventured out I kinda curled up in a convenient snowbank and had beavers offer me their waterproof coats. Well, I love winters and cold weather, but I hate being cold and miserable. A good shelter makes for good comfortable *living* out of doors.

If you find yourself without bedding, the debris shelter *is* your bedding. But don't make it your house, too. Build something to live in while you're up and about and can tend a fire. Use the litter for a sleeping bag.

Once you understand fairly well the basics of a shelter—what it's supposed to do, what its limitations are—then it'll be pretty simple to adapt the resources you have at hand and make a comfortable camp.

A special thanks to our friend Bill Lansdown of Alva, Oklahoma, who spent nine days with us while we constructed the shelters illustrated here. His strong back and ready wit were a tremendous help.

What a Shelter Keeps Out (and In)

A shelter is simply a barrier between you and whatever is *out there*. Wind, sun, heat, cold, rain, snow, bears…bears? No bears here. Let's stick to the weather—the elements.

From the above list, what we'll concern ourselves with here is protection from cold and wet. If you can get those under control, making barriers from the other elements (excepting maybe high winds) will be a piece of cake.

We need to keep the water out, and we also want to be able to have a fire in, or convenient to, the house—preferably inside. We'll be using strictly natural materials.

Although these "ideal" shelters will be constructed with the function of being able to have an inside fire, you must at every moment be aware of the real danger of *uncontrolled* fire. Remember always (and I'll remind you) that we're actually constructing an ideal tinder nest that *can go up in flames in only seconds*. Real care must be constantly taken with fire in shelters.

Shelter Basics

Six basic elements will pretty well cover any of our shelters: site, floor, walls, roof, smoke hole, and entrance. Let's discuss them one at a time.

Site

The location of our house should be the first thing to think about. What do we want it *near* to? And what do we want it *away* from?

Near to trees, bushes, rocks, whatever, to help add additional shelter to our shelter. Near to work sites. Near to water (but not in an area that might be prone to flooding if the water level rises). Near to building materials.

Away from tall trees or other high landmarks that may draw lightning. Away from unwanted sounds (like waterfalls) and sights. Away from any objects that may fall on us (such as dead tree limbs, or rocks from cliffs).

Once you've found the *general* location, look for *specifics* such as high spots. You'll want your wilderness house to sit higher than the surrounding land, in order to shed water. Finding the general location is usually much easier than deciding on the specific spot to build. Geri and I have spent as much time selecting sites as we have in actual building. Ideally, we want a small hillock just the size of our projected house. *This will send whatever rain that falls away from us.* This may seem a simple thing, but on many occasions we've witnessed small rivers running through someone's tipi at some of the rendezvous we've attended. The water has to go somewhere— and it always goes downhill. Digging a trench or building a retainer on the uphill side will sometimes divert water from your bed.

Floor

For all our shelters, the existing ground will be the floor. It may be padded with leaves, grass, dirt (if on rock), or some other material to your liking. We don't look upon the floor, as in modern structures, as something to keep litter free. Dirt comprises most all our house floors. Softer materials under bedding does make for better sleeping for your aching body, though. Primitives both today and yesterday often poured blood on the floor that then hardened and became rubbery, like linoleum. If required, or desirous, to build in a wet area such as a swamp, you can lay a network of poles over a framework to raise you up.

Walls

For protection from the sun alone, walls might not be needed. For protection from just about anything else, walls are a necessity. As we'll see shortly, the walls are often integrated into the roof *with the frame.* Sometimes, however, the walls will be separate. In many cases, the walls will also support the roof. Sometimes a single-thickness wall will do the trick, but more often than not, for the purposes intended here for protection from water and cold, a double-thickness wall is what we want. Wind and sun aren't all that hard to keep at bay. The interior temperature can be raised considerably with minimal protection. But water has a way of getting through almost anything eventually. So, if we can get our house waterproof, we've got it made.

We'll illustrate here how to incorporate and use rocks in one circumstance. What we find almost as simple to construct and highly effective, when using most materials, is a double row of sticks placed in the ground and filled with litter. This makes for a completely airtight, waterproof wall.

Roof

To us, the roof is one of the most critical segments in a shelter. It will usually be the one most responsible for keeping out the water, so here's where we'll give what seems to be the most attention. A roof is what makes a shelter.

For our criteria, the roof needs to repel water. Not a really simple task, but also not that difficult if you're aware of some basic rules.

Rule #1: Water runs down. Seems obvious, yes, but it's surprising how many forget this when building a shelter. Most rains are accompanied by wind that pushes the water in from the side. Once water hits the roof, the water will cease its sideways motion and begin to fall downward. What we need to do is slow this fall till it gets beyond the inside of our house.

With a flat roof, once the water hits, it has nowhere to go but into the house. Flat roofs don't work primitively unless we have a large rock outcropping or something similar. Mostly, forget about flat.

Now, *the steeper the pitch of the roof, the faster that water will run down it,* giving it less time to soak through the materials and come inside.

The *thicker* the roof covering, the more time it takes the water to penetrate it. The *finer* the material used in the covering, the longer it takes for the water to get through. Thus, coarser materials call for thicker coverings.

Long grasses make for good coverings. Water has a natural tendency to follow the stems and leaves of the grasses. Every time the water hits an obstruction, it will divert from its sideways following of the grass, and will fall to the one below it. So we need the material to be thick enough that, by the time it works its way around all the grasses and falls out the other side, it will be beyond our living space.

Place the grass upside down on the shelter. As water follows the stems and leaves, it will then naturally follow downward. If the grass is placed on the way that it grows, whenever water reaches the junction of leaf and stem, it will drip.

Smoke Hole

Since one major requirement here is the ability to use fire with (and within) our house, we'll need some method to allow the smoke to leave.

Smoke will naturally seep out of the roof of all these primitive shelters. We just can't get them completely airtight with the materials we have at hand, though leaving some other opening (if kept small) doesn't hurt. You'll see four methods in the pages to follow.

Keep the roof space high.

Rule #2: Smoke rises. If the interior ceiling is high, on days when the smoke seems to linger, it will be above your heads. In the shelters here illustrated using interior fires, in all cases when we've had fires, we've been able to stand comfortably, as the smoke was sufficiently ventilated. Smokier fires require more ventilation, so burn small-diameter, dry wood.

Entrance

We of course need some way in and out. It would also be proper to have some means of closing this off, such as a door.

Animal skins have been used as doors forever, whether raw or tanned. Large pieces of bark work too, as do grasses rolled into a ball, or even a piece of log.

Rule #3: If the lower walls are sealed tight, including the entranceway, you'll have less trouble with moving air, and with air moving smoke around the place.

House Materials

An unbelievably large amount of material is needed in constructing a good shelter. The material shown here made one simple wickiup.

One thing *not* to do is to limit your construction to specific materials. Learn to use to the best advantage *any* materials. Integrate. Mix and match.

When constructing a shelter to repel water, you'll want to work mostly with small, grass-sized material, which will compress better. Thicker stock such as sunflower stalks, willow, or dogwood shoots look good but require much thicker walls to repel water, as there's so much air space for the water to work its way through.

Try any of these materials:

✿ Sod	✿ Stone
✿ Dirt	✿ Grass
✿ Wood	✿ Leaves and litter
✿ Bark	✿ Lashing material

It is unbelievable, the amount of materials necessary to construct a good weatherproof shelter. The larger the size, the more material that's needed.

If the house is for long-term use, make it large enough for however many people *and* their supplies. The four shelters illustrated here are designed for three to four people. Smaller shelters are easier to heat. For interior fires, roofs must still be high.

Availability of materials should be real high on the site-selection list. It can be tedious and time-consuming to haul materials from any distance at all.

Is there a sequence in building? Well, probably most times. I suppose it might help to gather materials before you begin any construction, but then again many times we'll just begin with the actual building and use whatever we come across by way of materials.

Very seldom do we approach building with any actual plan in mind. We just want to end with the best shelter possible under the circumstances. Some might think that for an overnight shelter any old thing will do, but what if you get a goose-drowner rain?

The importance of the roof is stressed throughout this chapter. The foundation or the framework, or both, need as much attention, as they'll hold it all together.

Do the best you can with what you've got to work with. There's not much sense in spending a few hours in putting up a roof if it doesn't repel anything.

The Wickiup

Warm and comfortable, the wickiup is probably one of the quickest and easiest shelters to construct. Using any number of materials, it can be put up in as little as an hour or so if materials are at hand. It can be built to repel most water, and a *controlled* fire is possible inside.

The fresh-cut cattails had a tendency to slide down, so we used bark (lashed loosely) to help.

A solid tripod is a must, since it's the foundation for all that follows. A "Y" in one or more of the logs or branches is important to help lock the "Y," if no lashing is available.

We used three types of materials for covering this particular wickiup: weeds and cornstalks for one third the total, grasses and leaves (litter) for a third, and cattails for a third. These were applied 6" to 8" thick for the most part. Thicker is better.

The finished product. It stands 7' inside with a diameter of 9' (note Geri's head at the door) and will accommodate three comfortably, more in a pinch. This shelter can be made any size. A fire makes it cozy in a hurry, though remember to keep it small and attended.

The Lean-To

The second shelter that we illustrate here is also something of a quickie. This is the shelter that I pretty much grew up with in the Appalachians of southern New York State some 30 to 40 years back.

Now, in my estimation, the basic lean-to that most people are familiar with falls far short of qualifying as a real "house"-type shelter. By its nature, lean-to's are exposed in one or more directions to the mercy of the wind and any wind-driven elements.

But when you're on the trail and using it as a one-nighter, this drawback isn't quite as noticeable as it will then be (or should be) when built with its back to the wind, or, if fitted with sides, possibly quartering the wind somewhat.

The wind is a fickle thing. Generally it doesn't blow exactly straight from any one direction but constantly shifts directions a bit. This fact alone makes sides on your lean-to a must (remember that walls needn't shed water so much as wind). If you expect to call this shelter home for any period of time, a coupla variations will help considerably to add to your comfort.

You'll note in the accompanying illustrations and photos that we've indeed added substantial walls or sides to the lean-to. Also, we've extended these to swing to the front right and left, to help block the wind. In addition to this you'll be quick to note that we have constructed a wall of sorts to the front of all this by several feet so that the wind is thereby blocked from all directions. This leaves us with approximately a 2' corridor left and right to enter by, and the fire is placed right in the middle of what little remains of the open area directly in front of the shelter. In actuality, what we've done is construct a chimney for our fire.

In Kansas, we generally build our shelters with the back to the West, as that's the direction the prevailing wind comes from. In summer, though, we face slightly north of West, and in winter we try to face somewhat south of West as the seasonal winds shift accordingly. The day we built this lean-to, the wind was from the Northeast (preceding a storm). The benefit of the eastern wall was visible with the first fire, as the smoke was blown not into the shelter but up and over it.

The basic framework of lean-to's varies slightly. Here we constructed, though among trees, an entirely freestanding lean-to. There are a multitude of ways of putting it together.

*We first need front supports. These will be supporting the entire structure, so use stout materials. **Left:** We used a simple branched stick. **Right:** We used two straight sticks (lashed) to provide the "Y" we needed. In either case, more strength is obtained by driving the poles into the ground if possible, or supporting with rocks if necessary.*

Into the "Y" of both we placed poles running to the ground (or, as you will note in the photos to follow, onto a log to slightly raise the back).

Across these we placed three straight poles. From now on we can use crooked poles in the roof, and the ceiling will still remain flat.

Here we've placed several not-so-straight poles to tighten the roof a little.

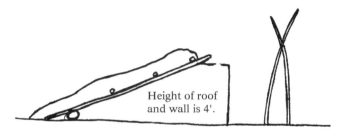

Height of roof and wall is 4'.

A view of the finished shelter from the side (South), illustrating relationship of actual lean-to size from front to rear (log at rear and top of roofline at front).

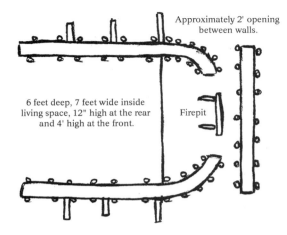

Approximately 2' opening between walls.

6 feet deep, 7 feet wide inside living space, 12" high at the rear and 4' high at the front.

Firepit

Bird's-eye cutaway view. The circles on either side of walls are sticks pushed into the ground, filled in between with sticks, grasses, leaves, weeds, and other litter to provide complete air-tightness (they support no weight).

Well, now that we've *sketched* it all out for you, let's go to the photos to see if this actually does work.

Initially, some time is spent finding the right site. Most important for us here is good drainage. Note that the site that Geri and Bill are looking over is slightly rounded.

Framing for the roof is complete.

Top: Framework for lean-to and walls is in place. East wall is half done.
Lower left: Close-up of wall under construction. Litter is compressed inward and down between sticks stuck in the ground to help form an airtight windbreak.
Right: Grasses and leaves being piled high onto roof. Walls are done.

Thatched Wickiup

With the first wickiup and the lean-to, we've made two of the quickest, easiest shelters to construct that go one or two steps beyond what most think of as "survival" shelters. In many true "survival" situations, naturally, you'd be just as well off (or better off) with one of the illustrated "houses" shown here.

But now let's take another step up the ladder in shelter construction. The framework for the wickiup to follow can be put together almost as quickly as the tripod shown earlier. The manner in which we'll apply the covering over most of the frame is where we'll advance.

More—actually, *much* more—time and effort will be spent in the initial gathering and preparation of materials. Here we'll be thatching, meaning tying bundles of grasses into place. This will require the use of more grass, as the bundles are compressed when they are tied in place. So, though this requires more time and energy to gather sufficient quantities, the resulting house will require less upkeep over time. The bundles will be as thick as you want (here a good 2") with three layers covering the whole as they're tied overlapping from the bottom up, as in shingling.

Some type of lashing material also needs to be considered. In the example shown on the following pages, we used basswood bark, which is simple and easy to both find and strip. (Many other materials are available. See pages 26-33.)

This style of house, in some form or fashion, has been used in most areas around the world where the necessary materials exist (just not, as far as I know, in the Arctic). In fact it's a common-style house in use still today in some of the remaining primitive cultures.

While this may seem to be a difficult project at first, as in many "difficult" projects the real "difficulty" lies in getting out and doing it. In actuality, once the materials were all in one place, the *putting together* took only about six hours' time, with three of us working.

So, let's do it.

Although we have good photos of the building process, maybe you'll get a better understanding of the all-important framework if we line draw some of it also.

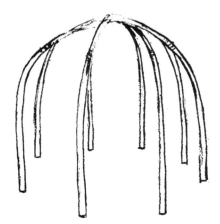

Step #1: Gather some green poles, somewhat longer than the intended shelter's height (here we used cedar). Stick the thicker end into the ground (several inches at least) in some semblance of a circle or oval or rectangle (no real rules here—your choice). Bend them over and where the opposing tops of pairs meet, lash them securely (they overlap by several feet).

Step #2: *At whatever spacing you desire (we used approximately 18"), lash horizontal poles into place. These not only add stability to the frame but are what we'll be lashing our thatching to. The bent door frame we just kinda stuck in (it need not be). We find that this limits the size of the opening, thereby cutting down drafts.*

Step #3: *Cover the entire frame completely with thatch. A good way to save on a lot of long thatching grass (and also create a completely airtight lower wall section) is to set shorter poles all around the framework about 6" out, also placing poles in between the existing uprights. (They can be spaced as close as you like. In fact, the closer together they are, the easier building you'll have, being able to use shorter and shorter materials.) The in-between area will be filled with litter. You can build the entire shelter in this manner, though the roof wouldn't shed water as well as the longer grasses do.*

Note the "pointy" top. This isn't necessary, but we find that it sheds water better. It's nothing more than three cedar limbs lashed together to two cedar "hoops." This uses the natural bend of the limb, and this all is lashed to the existing frame.

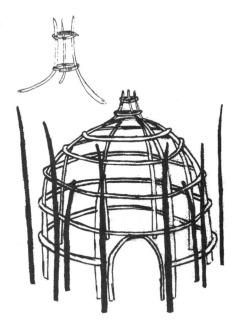

Building the framework.

Let's now take a photo journey while putting together this wickiup, to show more clearly some of the steps. The construction of the bottom portion of the wall can be accomplished in several ways, using many approaches—we show only one here. The entire structure could possibly be built even better if it all was done in this manner. This would also make it easier to find materials, as you wouldn't be limited strictly to long grasses (though the roof would repel water better if it had a finishing layer of thatching).

Finishing off the lower walls.

The actual job of thatching is not such a project as you might think. Gathering is
much more time-consuming. You do need to consider just what lashing you'll use.
Here we've used basswood bark. You might find it more convenient to splice the
lashing as you go, so that you end with one continuous cord rather than tying off
at the end of each length. Make one wrap around both horizontal pole and the
bunch of grass. The bark and grass will shrink somewhat (the grass especially,
if not dried), so retying may be necessary. The tighter together the bunches
are tied, the tighter the finished job. Stagger the thatching so that two thirds are
overlapping by the next layer; this way, the entire house will end with three coats.
Thatching begins at the bottom (as with shingles) so that moisture runs off the
upper layers onto, not into, the lower layer.

The piece we built to point *the top (inside and outside views).*

Note small size of entranceway in photo above (making it easier to close, but you'll have to crawl in here). The opening can be made to whatever size you desire.

Generic Shelter

We've now covered three different basic shelters—two of them quickie, or "survival," types. In the construction of them we've seen three varying frames and roof types, plus a simple way to build walls or sides.

When we build shelters, we usually have only a very basic concept in mind, certainly no blueprints. Terrain and materials are the two main guidelines.

With this next house we'll approach the job at hand with a single concept in mind: to use the rock face of one of our ravines to form at least one side of our house (or better yet, two sides).

One benefit of this approach is the fact that, obviously, part of your construction is already done, so you'll spend less time gathering building materials. Another is the fact that they're also placed below ground level so that you're additionally sheltered. Also, by placing your fire against the rock face, you'll store up heat by day to help warm you through the night when you don't want a fire burning (just like some houses these days use passive solar heating principles to warm tiles and walls).

One thing to remember with this trick, however, is that many ravines are the result of water runoff, and all of them are places where water *will* run. You certainly won't want to build in the middle of a possible river that the next rain will create. The secret here is to walk the edges of possible sites and look for places where water won't flow. If the ravines were made due to water running, they're still not excluded. Water won't run over all sides at every spot. In fact, it will usually be a problem only at a few key points. You usually won't have much trouble locating the dry streambeds to avoid. Flattened grass is one sign, worn down to the bedrock is another. You don't want to take shelter in your house during a rain, only to have it wash you away.

So let's take a walk through what we did here.

Site selection was the first consideration. Here Geri and Bill study the prospective site. The pluses: Rocks form two sides, for a good height of 2 1/2" or so, and runoff will be easy to divert. One minus: The long, open side faces north—nothing we can't overcome.

*Bill cleans up the future floor (**left**) by removing rocks and leveling the earth. He temporarily places the rocks in position close to where the final walls will end. The bird's-eye diagram (**below**) shows what the site was to begin with. Diagrams on the following pages clearly show the progress, especially when intermixed with the photos.*

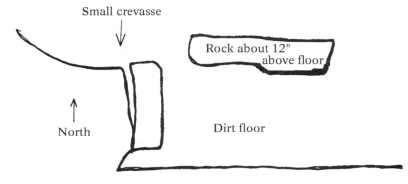

Small crevasse

Rock about 12" above floor

North

Dirt floor

Rock ledge 30" above floor

Rocks were laid to form a wall on the low sides (north and east) about 20" high. Grass was used as a bedding for the rocks so as to create an airtight seal.

On the ledge side most exposed (south), a berm of dirt and rocks was placed to help divert any runoff water (not so much from the surrounding terrain as from the south side of the roof itself, *left*).

A gap between the west and south walls serves as a natural ventilator, so we decide to build the fire area here, covering the top with flat rocks and mortaring them in place (using wet clay as mortar).

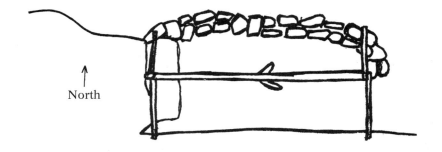

North

Note changes in bird's-eye drawing (**above**) from that on page 94. Rock wall laid on north and east sides. Main support rafter is in place, running the length, with upright supports at each end and in the middle. Ends are braced from the sides.

Geri places a flat rock on chimney as rain cap (**above**).

For the west wall (or gable), we choose to use sod, since its close proximity to the chimney will help to prevent possible fire.

Lashing together the framework.

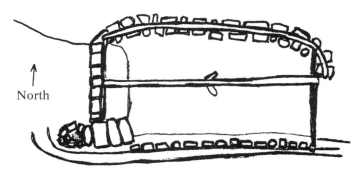

↑
North

*Sod wall in place on west (**left**), brace pole in place on north and east (**top**) to hold rafters. Chimney is in place, as is water-diversion berm on south (**bottom**).*

*Sod is placed onto the bottom of the south rafters to add to the water-diversion berm (**right**).*

Long grasses are placed on the roof, overlapping the sides and several inches thick. Some pieces of bark are placed on the very peak to help this vulnerable area to shed water.

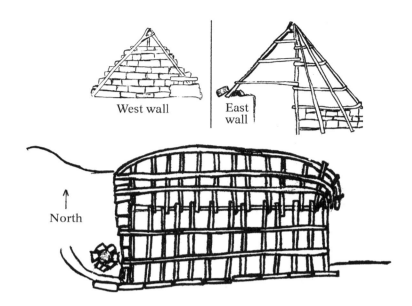

West wall

East wall

North

Addition of all rafters and horizontal cross ties. Sod placed on bottoms of south rafters for water-diversion berm. Roof is now ready for covering.

Large limbs are placed over the whole to secure it in winds.

Time to settle in.

Wrap-Up

So there you've got it—four different types of primitive, semipermanent shelters, using several methods of construction. Certainly not *one* set of rules or blueprints to follow.

What we hope to have accomplished here is to show you how to think a bit for yourself and use some field expedience when it comes to sheltering yourself in a wilderness or survival situation.

As with most primitive skills, *there's no one way of doing it.* We teach so that the student is capable of accomplishing the task at hand—successfully. We show characteristics, generically, so that you can use these skills in your own backyard, wherever that may be.

Use what you have, and do it *your* way.

Chapter 4

Makin' Meat – 1

I have found that many people who know of and talk, write, or teach some survival and wilderness skills will take their students through to a finished primitive product or skill from today backward, using today's technology to a primitive end. I was guilty of that myself in the first of my books—using nylon cords, steel blades, and so on. I've found that the reason that I am so rounded in my outdoor education (like others of my ilk) is that we taught ourselves these skills from nothing forward—how to go "naked into the wilderness" and manage to live.

The Primitive Bow and Arrow

One example: the primitive arrow. To go from nothing, forward, you first need some insight as to the type of wood to use—a knowledge, however simple, of working with stone tools to peel and smooth the shaft; of making fire so that the shaft can be heated and straightened; of working with cordage so as to apply the fletching and point. A step up from the most primitive of arrows requires the skills to work flint or bone to make a more serviceable point, then to apply them well. It also requires the knowledge of boiling down hide scrapings and other animal parts to make glue without the advantage of a pot. That's a lot of different skills needed for a single puny (but magnificent) arrow.

In this chapter I don't delve into sinew (it's covered in Chapter 10). The current chapter was, in its original concept, going to be just one chapter that covers some of the various methods of subsisting in the wilderness, beginning with the bow and arrow, but, well, I plain ran outta room. By the time I had finished the instructions on the primitive bow and arrow, I found that I had filled the allocated pages for one chapter. Therefore I wrote another one, Chapter 5, which goes into the use of snares, deadfalls, marine life, insects, and the like, so that one can subsist in the wilds.

I don't pretend to have enough knowledge of edible plants to even mention them. It's a skill that in itself requires years, if not a lifetime, of learning. Certainly, I have learned a little along these lines in the acquiring of other knowledge, but I can spend six weeks or less with an individual and teach him or her how to live *well* in the out-of-doors, including how to obtain sufficient sustenance to live. In that period of time I wouldn't even have my foot in the door when it comes to edible plants. To me, this knowledge would be nice to know—someday.

Now, the methods that I describe here are *mine*. They work for me. What I describe as cardinal rules, not to be ventured from, are broken all the time by a bowmaker friend of mine, whose bows work great. So what I describe isn't the *only* way—but they *do* work for me! And what I describe as happening to the wood at various stages may not be the reality for you. But if you approach the project thinking the way that I describe it, your finished product will be workable, and that's what counts.

We'll be using hand tools here—not the primitive tools that will be required in a strictly primitive situation, but modern "white man tools." The use of stone and bone for tools is covered in Chapter 2.

I'll also be throwing in ideas and tips that I've picked from various sources. What I put forth does work—though, as I stress, it's not the only way. In fact, throughout the entire book, I'll be showing you how to accomplish the task at hand, but will also keep the door open so that you may use your own ideas to come up with other, and quite possibly better, ways to accomplish the same end.

Anatomy of a Bow

Simply put, a bow is a stick with a string tied at each end that will propel an arrow. To understand how to successfully make this stick bend, time and again, to its full potential, we need a quick lesson in physics. So, pay close attention; this is important.

• Any piece of wood of equal dimensions from end to end will bend at the middle when force is applied. With a bow, the midsection moves in one direction, the two tips in the opposite direction. To counteract this, we remove wood from the limbs of our bow—more from nearer the tips than from closer to the grip.

• When removing wood while shaping and tillering a bow, one equation is of importance. If half the wood is removed in the *width* of the bow, the strength is halved. If one eighth of the wood is removed in the *thickness* of the bow, the strength is decreased by close to one half! What this shows is that the bow will be more effective if it's narrower and thicker, especially at the tips. (This is explained shortly.)

• The outside of the bend (back of the bow) will be trying to tear apart (tension). The inside (belly) will be compressing.

• *Most woods are stronger under tension than under compression.* The fibers of most woods will fail first under compression. This is followed almost immediately by the tearing apart of the back, leaving you with the false impression that the back failed first.

• Tillering, meaning equal bending of the limbs, is critical. If a portion of the limb isn't bending, somewhere else is bending too much—and failure can result.

• Somewhere toward the center (between back and belly) of this piece of wood is a neutral plane where no forces are in effect (at least, that we need be aware of here). From this neutral plane outward in each direction, all, or 100 percent, of the forces of tension and compression are being exerted. Simple, yes. *But*...the closer to the neutral plane, the less force exerted. So, how this affects us is that the nearer the outside (either side), the furthest from the neutral plane, is where most of the percentage of tension and compression is occurring. So, a higher percentage of tension and compression is taking place in a smaller percentage of the wood. Fifty percent of these forces are happening in the outer 10 percent of the wood. What that tells us is that a flat outer surface will make a stronger bow because this higher percentage of forces is spread over a wider surface. The backs of bows, we don't have that much control over; we need only follow the growth ring of the tree. The smaller the tree or limb, the rounder the outer surface, and the more tension exerted in a smaller area. But the belly we *do* have control over. That, we can make flat. And since the majority of woods fail first under compression, this works to our advantage.

• Mass of the wood—the actual bow itself—slows down the working action or response and so directly affects the performance of the arrow. This is most noticeable toward the tips of the bow. So, the less mass (wood/weight) for a particular weight bow, the better the performance.

• Each piece of wood has its ideal width-to-thickness ratio. Generally speaking, the harder the wood, the narrower this is. The narrower that you can make your bow, the more effective it will be because it will contain its least mass. Less mass means faster performance. *But...*

• What we're after in our chosen piece of wood is the ratio whereby the bow can be bent to its fullest extent (at a point somewhere around half its length), *and* to have this wood not fail under either tension or compression (all woods will fail if pulled too far). Let's assume our wood is stronger under tension and that we have an unviolated back. All we need concern ourselves with now is compression. *All* woods will fail under compression, to some extent. Our ideal bow will fail only slightly noticeably. Assuming that we're working with a straight bow, this is the stage we want our bow to be in at this point in time. Each wood will be different, just as each round from the same tree will also differ somewhat. There's no set formula. A hardwood, such as Osage orange, will reach this stage, being thicker and narrower than a comparable piece of, say, hickory (another hardwood).

• If a straight bow is made to this perfection, with the same length and weight (let's say 48" and 55 lb, and with the specific gravity, (weight) being about equal, the narrower, thicker bow will shoot farther and faster because it will contain less mass (2:1 compared to 8:1).

This knowledge hasn't just appeared to me in dreams but has come from many sources, some even the aforementioned books. But the largest contributors to making my mind think "bows" have been *Jeff Schmidt*, a professor of physics whose workings with the Asian composite bow have enlightened me as to the physics involved, and *Tim Baker,* who has done the most extensive research and testing of the primitive bow of anyone I know. To both these fine folks, my thanks for their completely unselfish sharing of information.

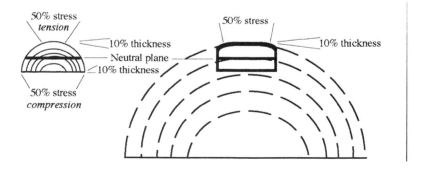

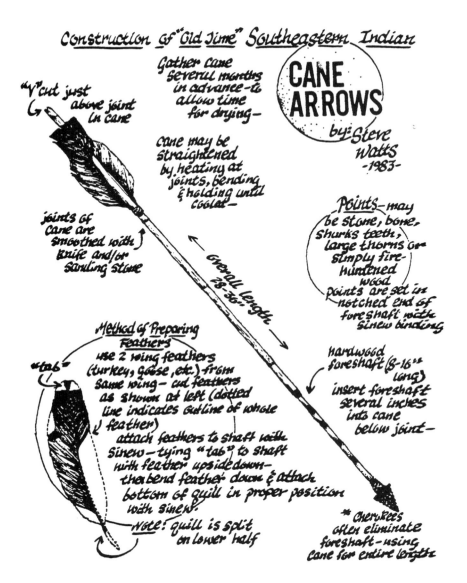

Construction of "Old Time" Southeastern Indian

CANE ARROWS

by: Steve Watts
-1983-

"V" cut just above joint in cane

Gather cane several months in advance—to allow time for drying—

Cane may be straightened by heating at joints, bending & holding until cooled—

joints of cane are smoothed with knife and/or sanding stone

Overall length 28-36"

Points—may be stone, bone, sharks teeth, large thorns or simply fire-hardened wood. points are set in notched end of fore shaft with sinew binding

hardwood foreshaft (8-16" long) insert foreshaft several inches into cane below joint—

Method of Preparing Feathers
use 2 wing feathers (turkey, goose, etc.) from same wing— cut feathers as shown at left (dotted line indicates outline of whole feather)
attach feathers to shaft with sinew—tying "tab" to shaft with feather upside down—then bend feather down & attach bottom of quill in proper position with sinew.
note! quill is split on lower half

"tab"

* Cherokees often eliminate foreshaft—using cane for entire length

A flyer borrowed from Steve Watts of Gastonia, North Carolina, on construction of old-time Southeastern Indian cane arrows

The Primitive Bow

Here I'm going to cover the wooden "self" (all one piece) bow, and the same bow backed with sinew. We'll end up with a short, sinew-backed bow common to the Plains Indians of North America. Since I go to all the trouble of making them, not only do I make them usable but also make them to be hung in a museum or the home of the discriminating collector. Most of my bows are in the 55 to 60 lb. range with a 20" to 22" arrow, and that's what we'll make here. You can make yours heavier or lighter.

Tools

Once the staves are prepared, for which I'll use a saw, a sledge, some type of heavy knife, and wedges, the only tools that I'll work with in the actual making of the bow will be a drawknife, a wood rasp/bastard file, and a pocketknife. Can't get much simpler than that. A vise is handy but not necessary.

Material

Almost any wood will make a bow, but there certainly are preferences. I have read of *willow, cottonwood,* and *sycamore* being used by some early Indians—not out of preference, but because of availability. I've made a few myself from cottonwood and willow that work well for rabbits in particular. I know from experience that *Osage orange* makes one of the best bows, with *yew* a close competitor. *White oak* makes a real fine bow, and it's a bit easier to work than Osage. The bow that we'll make here will be *hickory*—not one of the better woods (it hasn't as much snap

as the others) but one that I highly recommend for the beginning bowmaker. It's a truly forgiving wood and almost impossible to break. You'll feel a lot of frustration when a bow breaks, so you might want to work with more of a sure thing on your first try. The steps illustrated here apply to all woods.

The list of preferred woods really isn't long. *Ash, black locust, lemonwood,* and *mulberry* are some of the others. But what was available is what was used in days gone by.

Generally the softer, more brittle woods (*yew, cedar*) were made into wide, flat bows and the harder and denser woods (*Osage, white oak*) made into narrow, thick bows.

Finding the Stave

The perfect stave would be straight, knot free, and resilient; would spring back to its original shape when unstrung, not staying bent (following the string); and would be snappy, kinda like spring steel. A lot to ask for in one piece of wood.

I cut most all my staves green, in the dead of winter when the sap's down (excess moisture takes longer to cure and leads to more checking and cracking). Occasionally I find a dead limb or tree that's ready to work in one of the hard or dense woods, though not often.

I want the stave as straight as possible, though they can be heated and straightened to a great extent later on.

I watch for knots. Best if there are none, but I've made several good bows by working around them, which will be explained later.

I take limbs or trunks of any size 2 1/2" or thicker. You could get by with smaller, but I like the extra freedom of material to work with. With the smaller size, I only try to get one good stave from the round, as it's not all that easy to split the smaller staves exactly in half. By carefully splitting the larger pieces I can get several staves from them.

Curing

I've read and heard of as many ways to cure out a stave as I've heard of making bows. Some folks bury them in their gardens, from six months to six years. Some cover the ends, or the entire log, with wax, allowing the log to cure slowly and minimize warpage and cracking…and on and on. I've also heard that it's best not to use kiln-dried wood.

Now, here's some of my own thinking. Green wood won't work, as its green, wet cells are especially weak under compression and fail immediately when bent, and also it's too slow in response to cast an arrow. The drier the wood, the faster (snappier). Too dry makes the wood too brittle, leading to breakage. So we need something in between.

The heavier dense woods need longer to cure than the looser-grained woods. The densest and heaviest include Osage and white oak. The other extreme includes yew and cedar, with most somewhere in between—like our model, hickory.

I take *all* my staves and debark them, then right away I split them into the size of stave that works out best. When debarking, take great care so as to *not* cut through the outer growth ring. In fact, it's wise to leave the slightest bit of inner bark on the stave to ensure this. I then split to separate the heart (inside) wood from the sap (outside) wood. The heart is denser and therefore dries at a different rate than the sap, which is a major cause of warpage and cracking. Sometimes I can save for usable staves both the heart and the sap woods, but more often I must choose.

With hickory I find that the sapwood is thicker than the heart, so I usually save the sap. With white oak I save the heart, and the same with Osage. (I know of one bowmaker who leaves the sap of Osage on the heart, which is only about 1/4" thick or less, as it acts as a sort of lamination, allowing for more flexibility.)

When splitting out the staves, with the bark off I can more easily see the knots and how the grain of the wood flows. This dictates precisely where to split. Knot free if possible, though knots in the center of the wood are not

much of a problem, unlike knots in the grip portion. Knots close to the edge should be avoided if possible (more on that later). Let the piece of wood that you're working with dictate the working of the bow.

If there's an average to the size of my staves, they would be about 1 1/2" thick by about 2 1/2" wide by however long. All either wood of the heart or the sap. These I'll hang in a covered area out of doors for about six to eight weeks; then I'll take them in by the fire for about another two to four weeks. Finally, I make bows from them.

I have successfully made bows from Osage, white oak, and hickory in as short a time from cutting as this.

Making the Bow

Now let's take hold of our cured stave. Plan to spend some time with it. Feel it. Look it over very carefully. Study it.

The rules to remember now are to (1) work with the grain, following it from one end of the stave to the other, and (2) *never* cut through the outside (back, or the side away from the shooter) growth ring. This I stress as a must, though I know of at least one bowmaker who always breaks this rule. If the ring happens to be cut through, remove the entire ring down to the next. Otherwise, this is where the bow is most liable to break. (3) Keep the knots to the inside of the bow. When a knot can't be avoided at the edge, *do not cut through the natural flow of the fibers around it.* Leave a bit of a bump there, which will just add character to the finished product. Cutting through the fibers will only weaken the limb at this point (a good friend of mine, another bowmaker, says exactly the opposite).

When studied long enough, the bow will "appear" to you within the stave. Follow the line of longitude grain and begin placing knots where they'll do no harm, eliminating all that you can. Is a narrow, thick bow called for, or one that's wide and flat? Every piece of wood speaks to you differently, and no two bows will be exactly alike. Take a pencil and draw an outline of your bow, making the center grip a bit longer than your hand is wide. When you've searched out the best possible section for a bow, looked it over from all sides, and drawn your outline, then you're ready to pick up the drawknife.

It's easiest to work with the aid of a vise, though I have free handed some and have also come up with several contraptions to work in the wild.

I normally first work the sides of the stave to the outline that I've drawn, though each piece will be different. I try to do this first, because when I begin working on the thickness of the limbs I can more accurately judge the weight of the bow and feel the bend of the limbs if it's almost to its proper width. At this point, keep the entire bow slightly oversized so that when it's heated to bend, if inadvertently scorched, there'll be room to remove some. Once the width is within 1/8" or so, begin working on the belly. Remember, *no more is to be removed from the back!*

I'll begin shaping with the grip. Just do whatever feels good to you. It's best to keep it thicker here then in the limbs so there'll be no bend, which

will cause it to kick. But careful study of old bows shows that, for the most part, Indians didn't worry much about this. The limbs should taper gradually from the grip to the tips. Work it slowly. Remember, once it's removed, it can't be put back. Once I get to within about 1/4" the final size, I'll put aside the drawknife and take up a wood rasp, as occasionally the knife will take a bit larger bite than I want. As the limb gets within bending range, slow down and feel your way carefully. Try to remove from the entire limb at the same time. When it begins to show bendability, back away from the grip and work only the rest of the limb, and so on till you get to the tip. At this stage, the limb should bend pretty evenly between the nock and the grip, but will still be much too strong to even consider stringing. When one limb is about where you want it, repeat with the other. The second limb will be more difficult, as you'll be trying to match the first. Simply work slowly, a little at a time. Keep a constant check on your progress by bending the bow over your knee. You don't need to be exact—eyeball it, as this isn't the finished size yet.

Now, before you get too confused as to some of the terminology that I'm using here, I'll include a short glossary of terms that I use.

Note deep cut caused by careless use of the drawknife. It's best to go slow and easy, leaving a lot for the wood rasp to do.

The *back* of the bow is the side that's away from you when the bow is strung, and the *belly* is the side facing you. The *grip* is the center of the bow that you grip when shooting. The *limb* is the section on either side of the grip running to the *tip*. The *ears*, if a bow has them, are the 4" to 6" at each tip that are bent back away from the belly, in effect shortening the bow. *Notches* are the depressions cut near the tips to hold the string.

Study carefully the series of photographs below and on the next two pages, which will take you from the raw stave through to the bow prepared for the first heating session.

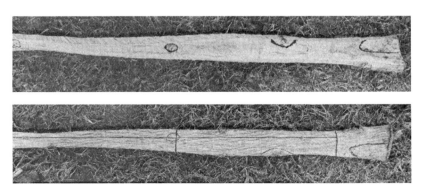

Heating and Bending

Once you've got the limbs bending pretty uniformly, it's time to do any bending of the bow that you may need or want to achieve. Seldom do I begin with a perfectly straight stave, as I usually save my best to sell, making my own bows from the harder-to-work pieces.

Many bows that I've worked have required straightening, which will be the first step. Once I get a straight bow, then I can decide how I want to bend it to shape. Sometimes, I leave it straight. Most often I'll reflex the bow (bend it in the opposite direction), because all woods will initially follow the string somewhat, especially hickory. I often will bend the ears back also, but the purpose of this is to shorten the bow and make it faster, and here we're already working with a short bow.

I once put ears on a beautiful Osage bow that I made, a nice, 42" bow. Afterward, I had to thin the ears to allow them to bend, because all the bend was forced into one small area of the limbs. I had already sinewed the back and so was unable to heat and straighten it.

The actual heating of the wood is done slowly. It can be done over an open fire, hot coals, the flame of a gas range, or even an electric range. The idea is to heat the fibers of the wood *completely through*. I apply grease (polyunsaturated bear grease, meaning Crisco) liberally on the spot that I'm heating. I've even tried steaming it, which takes much too long. I've heard of others who use water in lieu of grease. Some even boil it. To my way of thinking, the grease or water serves two purposes: (1) to help protect the wood from scorching, which will make the wood brittle and worthless, and (2) to allow moisture (in the form of steam?) to penetrate the fibers of the wood. Whether that's so or not, that's the way I look at it. Whatever, it does work.

When the fibers are heated completely through, the wood will bend as easily as it does when green. *But,* if kept in its new position till it cools, it will pretty much stay there. You must be careful and not overdo it. It's easy enough to take it too far and tear or break the fibers. You'll have to feel this as you go. Heat, bend a little, reheat, bend some more—when it breaks, you've gone too far! I've never had a piece break while doing this.

Some bowmakers make a jig and place the bow into it till it's completely cooled. I just hold it in position for about 30 to 45 seconds, and it seems to stay pretty close to where I want it. Keep the piece *moving constantly* over the fire, never letting it stay exposed to the heat at any one spot for too long, which will lead to scorching. (The purpose of leaving the bow oversized till now was to give something extra to remove in the event that it got a bit scorched.) If I'm wanting to bend only a small area, I'll heat an area about

3" to 4" long. If the bend or twist (yes, twists can be eliminated if they're not too bad) is spread over a longer area, heat it all. In about 3 to 5 minutes, a small area should be hot enough to bend, depending on the thickness. I can't overstress the importance of not scorching. Go slow.

Note scorch, the reason for leaving oversized (brittle portion will be removed).

Now, another important point: Heat and bend an area on one limb. If there's a spot that you can also work on the other limb that won't interfere with the spot that you've just bent (straightened), do it also. Then lay it aside till it has a chance to *completely* cool. If you try to do too much at one time, areas that have already been worked, but are still warm within, can easily get accidentally rebent. Bending isn't something to be done at one sitting. Some of my bows take several days to get to where I'm satisfied with them, so don't get overanxious.

I take the bow to straight first (unless a natural bend can be used advantageously in the finished shape of the bow), and then I do whatever shaping I deem necessary. I have read, and heard from several sources, that if one part of a bow is heated, you should do the same spot on the other limb—but I don't bother about that.

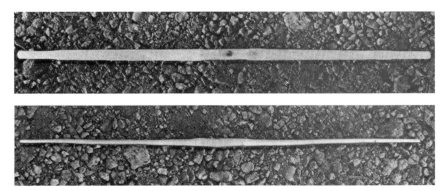

Bow taken to straight.

Final Working

When all the heating, straightening, and bending is done, now's the time to get down to the nitty-gritty of finishing your project.

With rasp in hand, approach the bow cautiously. You're going to carefully remove wood to the final size—very slowly, so as not to overdo it. Remember, it can't be put back.

Usually, but not always, the grip will need no further work. If, however, it was left oversized, for the purpose of straightening or whatever, start there. Work it down till you have what you want. Don't just jump in and start filing away, though, but look it over from all sides and remove wood so that things stay uniform.

Final shaping and bending (tillering) should be done cautiously, slowly, bit by bit. I work one limb at a time, rasping or scraping gently with a steel blade held at an angle of 90° (plus or minus) to the belly of the limb. I sweep the entire length, from grip to tip. *The thickness of the limb should be getting thinner, the farther out toward the tip you go. This is a must!*

Also, I've found that some students read or hear me say that the belly needs to be flat the entire length of the limb—and rightly so. But don't misinterpret this to mean that you can ignore the shape of the bow's back. If the back sways south, so goes the belly. The final limb may appear like a rough road, but it *must match the back in thickness*.

Bend the bow to test it, by placing the tip on the ground and applying backward pressure at the grip. Watch the bending. You don't want to see any one area bending. If you do, it means that excess stress is being placed there, so you must remove material from areas above, below, or both to even out the bend. Most every time it'll be visually apparent that areas are thicker or thinner, simply by looking from the side. Running your hand down the limb, thumb on the belly and fingers on the back, will often feel thicker or thinner areas. Take your time.

All material is to be removed from the belly. Leave the back (one growth ring) alone! Do the other limb till it looks and feels the same. Many times, that's all I need to do to now string the bow.

The last few paragraphs won't take but a minute to read, but, in the doing, expect to spend the better part of a day to do things right.

Remember that, when finishing, you're going to remove any scorched areas (except from the back; if you have scorched here, it'd be best to remove one entire growth ring and start over). Scorched areas are brittle and will break easily. We're going to be tillering the limbs, but *we're not gonna touch the back of the bow!*

Carefully removing just a little at a time.

When we're satisfied, now's the time to cut our nocks for the string and to string the bow. Here, any *strong* cord will suffice. (Strings will be covered soon.) The cuts for notches can be done about any way that you like. They need only be near the tip of the limbs, suitable to hold the string. Many old bows had no nock at all, just a buildup of sinew to prevent the string from sliding down the shaft. The photos show the way that I do mine. Old bows were done in many ways. The most common method of the Plains Indians was to put two nocks on the lower end of the bow and one on the upper (maybe to allow them to move the string line of sight to one side of the grip or the other). This is what I normally do.

The bow, before final heating and finishing, draws 50 lb. at 15 1/4".

Series showing steps in bending. In all photos, belly is up.

#1—Both limbs reflexed at grip

#2—Toward the tips curved back in

#3—Bow now strung, tested 45 lbs. at 22" draw

#4—Showing how bow somewhat followed string from just one time stringing

If we've watched what we're doing up till now, the limbs should be fairly close. Now I'll make use of a tillering board. This can be as simple as a heavy nail or spike driven into an upright post or board, to hold the center (grip) of the bow, with nails placed at about 2" intervals below it. With this, you can put a loose string on the bow and stress the limbs very little by pulling the string down a nail at a time and paying attention to how each limb bends, both individually and as a matching pair. At the point the limbs are bent, if you see a problem area you can immediately stop and touch up that spot. Once the bow's bent far enough that the string at the grip area is at the proper height (test by running another string or straight stick from tip to tip), you can then stop and string the bow to the proper height. For most longer bows, that height is about 6"—the height of a fist with a thumb sticking up. For my own bows of 44" or less, I make it just fist-high (about 4"). This is called the *brace height.*

I'll continue pulling the string one nail at a time till I feel I'm stressing too much, and then will remove wood from both limbs. I do this by feel, and many times my bow will break, as I'm trying to make it too heavy a draw weight for the wood it's made of. Most times, I'll quit long before I reach the 2:1 ratio (half the length of the bow), then I'll shoot it a lot to kinda break it in, hoping to gain an inch or two. Most good bowyers "overbuild" their bows—meaning that they create one at the magic 2:1 ratio without coming close enough to the breaking point to worry about it. (I'm not that smart.)

The first thing I do after stringing for the first time is to pull easily to "feel" how it pulls. With the short bows that I make, I use an arrow about half the bow's length, usually 20" to 22". I'll use a premeasured stick or an arrow to check this. The short bows "stack up" quite fast (by stacking up, I mean that they suddenly get harder and harder to pull). Pull gently at first. Now's a good (or bad) time to break it. Feel it out. If the wood suddenly feels like it won't give any more, listen to it. Remove some more wood *from the belly* to limber it.

Checking bendability of bow constantly as we go.

With most of my bows, I like to end at this stage with about a 45 lb. pull at what I've decided the arrow length to be. This I measure by pulling from a scale. Whatever the scale reads at the full draw length is what I call the bow weight. I don't know how the "big boys" do it. Bows can be made to pull at whatever weight you desire, but since I back all of mine with sinew I keep it at about 45 lbs. here. The two layers of sinew that I'll apply will bring the bow, after final tillering, to 55 to 60 lbs.

At this point we have a finished, shootable, self bow of about 45 lbs. draw weight with a 22" arrow.

If we were to keep it here and not go on to sinew it, it would call for some sort of sealing to protect it from the elements. In the old days, grease was liberally applied, and reapplied, and even some more, for the purpose of keeping the bow limber. Most times, the bow would be heated somewhat and then the grease (and maybe brains) applied.

My thinking, again: If kept in the moisture, unprotected, for long, the wood would soak up moisture and become weaker and subject to rot. If kept unprotected in a low-humidity area, it would dry to the point that it would become too brittle and therefore subject to breakage.

Whatever, you can stop here if you want. I never do. Next for me is to...

Back the Bow with Sinew

Remember what I said earlier about the ideal bowstave having the quality of springing back to its original shape when unstrung? Well, many woods don't possess that quality. In fact, the hickory bow that has just been made is one of the worst for "following the string." It wouldn't be long before the bow would be bent almost to the point that it would require no additional bending to string it. This problem for me arises by my making the bow narrow, trying to replicate a Plains Indian piece. It would be tempered or eliminated if I made the limbs wider and therefore spread the stress over more area.

Applying sinew to the back of the bow will help greatly in reducing this tendency. It will also add strength, power, and "snap." Beyond that, it will add greatly to the bow's elasticity. On some bows where I haven't reached the desired draw length but haven't wanted to shave away any more wood, I've gone ahead and sinewed and then have been able to increase the draw. The application of sinew really does a lot for the tension of wood.

Three strips of deer sinew, two partially separated.

Read through this section thoroughly, and understand it completely before proceeding. This step is kinda complicated to describe, even with the help of photos, yet the actual process of sinewing is really much easier than describing it. When you understand precisely what you're doing, why you're doing it, with what you're doing it, and how to do it, the actual "doing" will be a piece of cake. Remember, also, that here we're working in the kitchen. It's really not all that much more difficult to do in the wilds, just much more time-consuming.

Sinew is tendon. It's available from all animals, including us. It can be taken from the legs or, preferably, from either side of the backbone. The sinew from the legs works, but is shorter by far than the loin sinew, and for this reason I don't use it, though I do keep some on hand. The much longer strips, one lying on either side of the backbone, are a lot more pleasant to work with and are easily enough removed from the carcass of any large animal. (See the "Sewing with Sinew" section in Chapter 10.)

Leg sinew must be pounded thoroughly and then separated into threads. The loin sinew, if cleaned properly, has only to be roughened between the fingers first (we're talking about 2 or 3 minutes' work here) and then separated into threads. I try to keep the threads all about a good 1/8" thick. I've found that three average loin strips of deer sinew will allow me to apply two coats to the bow and have enough left over for the bowstring. The entire process of preparing the threads takes little more than an hour.

To prepare the bow, it must be washed thoroughly. *All* grease and oils must be removed for the glue and sinew to adhere, and that includes the oils from your hands. Some wash their bows with lye. I did on two bows, though I didn't like working with the caustic stuff and went back to my method of a good scrubbing. A toothbrush works well, with Ivory dish soap and lots of *hot, hot, hot* water, then rinsed very thoroughly. Also wash the belly of the bow for a couple of inches down from both tips. The bow can be sinewed either damp or dry; I've found no difference. Now, *don't* touch the back of the bow with your hands again till you're applying the glue.

Also, the nap of the wood on the back of the bow must be raised so that the glue has something to adhere to. This can be accomplished with either a file or a hacksaw blade, working gently so as to barely raise the nap. Don't go so deep that you cut through the growth ring. This can be done either before or after the washing.

Glue

Here I'm going to break one of my rules and make a statement that I haven't personally tested to see whether it's true, though it's the consensus of all bowmakers I've spoken to. "Sinew is protein. The only glue that can successfully be used with it is another pure protein—meaning glue from hide." This makes sense to me, and *hide glue* is all I've ever used with sinew. And it does work. I haven't tried any of the other commercial glues available. Sinew isn't all that easy to come by, and I don't want to take the chance of ruining any. I've always had access to glue from hides, or have taken the time to make it.

As the name implies, hide glue can be made from hide. Simply boil a hide in water long enough, and glue will be extracted from it into the water. If the hide is in small pieces or scrapings (or both), it will happen faster, since it has more surface area. Bring a pot of water to a boil and add the makin's (hide scrapings, sinew scrapings, cartilage, and so on). This is often referred to as *hoof glue,* though in fact the horny parts of hooves can't be boiled into glue—they're the wrong stuff. When hooves are thrown into the pot, any glue produced would have come from cartilage. Anyhow, boil away. After some time (maybe hours for larger pieces), the glue stuff will be extracted into the water. The glue can be made thicker now by further boiling. We've found that making it on hot rocks (depressions) or in ceramic pots in field work is convenient for not-so-refined glue. When making it at home or under more controlled conditions, it would be better to keep the liquid thinner. Strain this through a filter of sorts (such as layers of cheesecloth) and then pour out in thin layers (on cookie sheets covered with tin foil: primitive here). The water will evaporate and leave thin sheets of glue behind. Keep this layer thin so that the water is allowed to evaporate more quickly (nothing smells quite as bad as rotting protein!), which is the reason for the flat sheet in lieu of a bowl. Leave it in sheets, or pulverize it for storage and when ready to use it add water and heat.

Hide glue can also be bought. Making it can be a real pain, and time-consuming (being hypocritical now, ain't I?), so I tend to buy most of what I use. It's available either granulated, as I just described, or in liquid form. I made several bows years ago using this liquid stuff. It worked, but took forever to cure out and always seemed tacky. I read in D. C. Waldorf's book *The Art of Making Primitive Bows and Arrows* that this was due to an additive and that it could be counteracted by adding vinegar. I tried that once but still didn't like working with it. It's not easy to find the granulated glue at times, though. You might try art supply stores and especially places that work with stained glass. A pound of glue will make three, four, or even more bows, with plenty of leftovers for arrows and other crafty things.

Now that we've got all the components together—sinew threads, hide glue, and the prepared bow—let's get going. I'll explain my setup and you can devise whatever will work best for you.

I work with two dishpans. One pan holds the bow for easy workability, back side up. In it I put about 1 1/2" to 2" of *cold* water to soak the sinew threads. Begin by soaking about one third (one loin strip) of your threads (assuming that you've used three deer loin sinews), or whatever. I like to soak them for several minutes. They become elastic when soaked and shrink as they dry, thereby adding their strength to the bow. *Hot* water will cook them, *warm* water will cause them to curl.

While these soak, add several cups of boiling water to a handful or so of the hide glue crystals in the second, smaller pan. This is variable, and you don't want it too watery but also not too thick, just like a thin syrup. After a lot of stirring, the glue will eventually dissolve in the boiling-hot water. You can speed this by first soaking in cool water.

The working temperature of the glue should be about 115° to 120°F, barely warm to the touch. The glue will set up fast at roughly 85° to 90°F.

I find working at a room temperature of roughly 85°F about right. I prefer it to set up kinda quick. The hotter the room, the slower the setup time. Therefore, you might find it easier working during the cold of winter when the room temperature is easier to control than on a 75° to 80°F day.

Place the pan holding the now-liquid glue into a third, somewhat larger pan containing *hot* water, such as a double boiler, to keep it at a good working temperature. Although the hands, bow, and glue would stand hotter temperatures, the sinew won't, so keep it just warm enough.

Put newspapers under it all, as things are about to get real sticky.

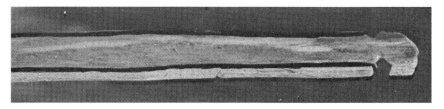

End of bow coated with glue and one thread "ridging" the outside. I inked in a ridge thread to make it show.

First, apply one or two coats of glue to the back of the bow, and allow to become tacky. The purpose now is to cover the entire back of the bow with an even layer of sinew threads, one thread deep. Try to avoid having bunches of threads meeting at the same "joint" (butt to butt), as in laying brick or stone; instead, overlap the threads. One by one, take each thread from the water, squeeze the excess moisture out of it between thumb and forefinger, dip it into the glue, squeeze out the excess between thumb and forefinger, and finally dip it into the glue once more and again squeeze out the excess (if the thread is left to soak in the glue, it'll begin to cook or curl). Now lay the thread onto the back of the bow. I begin by placing the first threads along the very edge of the bow, from one end to the other, going through whatever nock there may be and on to the other side. If there is no nock, as in my one-nock end, then go over the tip and down the other side for a few inches.

When applying this first layer of sinew, I prefer to make this "ridge" on either side of the bow, as it serves as a guideline, making it easier for me to evenly fill the space in between. I know of others who count each thread to make certain that an equal number is placed on each limb. For this first layer, it's not necessary. The entire back needs to be covered, for the best result. If the bow is tillered pretty close, the limbs should be about equal widths anyhow. The only way that you might run into trouble is by placing threads of varying sizes on the opposite limbs. If the threads are fairly close, you'll have no trouble.

You'll note that I said to run the threads over the tips and down the other side a coupla inches. If there's to be more than one coating, this wouldn't be necessary at this time (though I do all mine this way). But with the final layer, the threads are carried over and then held in place by wrapping with a sinew thread, to keep the ends from pulling loose.

I invariably apply two coats of sinew to my bows. After the first is in place, I take a 15- to 20-minute break to allow the first to set up somewhat. Also, now should be about the time to begin soaking more threads, if you haven't had to do so by now. For the second layer, I usually don't use quite as much sinew as I did in the first, unless I'm trying to add power to a particular bow.

For this layer, I count the threads: 12 on one limb, 12 on the other. These threads are all placed down the center of the bow, not as an even layer like with the first. The threads will spread out as you apply them, and the finished appearance will be slightly rounded. From one to three dozen threads to each limb should do the trick here. Remember *not* to butt the ends, but to overlap, and also to carry the threads over the tips and down the other side a bit.

You'll find that you'll have to replace the *hot* water in your tray once or twice, to keep the glue at its proper temperature. You'll also find globs of glue building on the bow, caused by the glue's cooling. Just wet your fingers in hot water and run them over the globs to smooth and remove them.

I use the pan of cool water (holding the bow and soaking the threads) to rinse my fingers as I go along, which is often. And it's a smart idea to keep old rags or paper towels handy to wipe with, not Ma's good towels.

When I'm satisfied with the job, I then smooth the entire surface with fingers dipped in hot water. At the tips and at all "low" spots, where the threads might have the tendency to pull loose while drying, take a sinew thread and tie it down.

The threads can be overlapped at the grips all they may. It won't hurt a thing, as there's no bend there.

Take the sinewed bow and hang it from pegs or nails and leave it be. Here in northeast Kansas with its high humidity, I leave it for two weeks to cure. On a coupla bows that I made in the deserts near Las Vegas, I was satisfied with the cure in one week. The color of the sinew will lighten noticeably as it dries.

Don't even be tempted to try to pull the bow and see how it's doing, *before* you're sure that it's cured. You'll only succeed in breaking the all-important bond between glue and wood.

The freshly sinewed bow.

When it's cured, you'll find that the drying, shrinking sinew has pulled the bow back—and that's good. With Osage or white oak, that's where it would remain. With our hickory, it will still "follow the string" slightly, but not near as much as if we hadn't sinewed it.

When first pulling the bow, and probably for some time afterward on the first few pulls, the glue will audibly crack. This will never cease to worry you!

When cured, the bow might need some final tillering. If everything had worked perfectly and the tillering was right on, you'd be in good shape. But most probably you'll have to loosen one limb or the other. String the bow and pull it a few times, then lay it down and eyeball or measure it. If one limb bends more than the other, cut any sinew ties that may be in the way and carefully scrape or sand some wood from the *belly* of the *stiffer* of the limbs. Do this with the bow unstrung. Remove only a little and then string it, pull the bow a few times, and finally check it again. When both limbs are equal (or close), the bow's all but done.

Some folks take the tillering to a more critical point. Using a board with notches cut into it about 2" apart, they place this board on the grip of the bow and move the string up a notch at a time, tillering at each step, till the draw length is reached. I've found that if the bow seems closely tillered as I've stated, it will look good all the way out. At least I've had no problems.

On one hickory bow that I made several years ago, I got to tillering and really overdid it. What began as a 55 lb. bow, because of overtillering first one limb and then the other, ended up as a 35 pounder. Instead of taking an ax to it as I was sorely tempted to do, I let it sit for several weeks while I calmed down. Then I simply resinewed it—a lot—and ended up with a fine-shooting 55 lb. bow. So much for the power of sinew!

OK. The bow has been sinewed, cured, and tillered. Now take a knife or some sandpaper and go over all unsinewed parts of the belly and sides to remove any remnant of glue (just to make it pretty). Also, replace any ties that you removed while tillering.

But now something has to be done to protect the bow. Not only the wood (of which I spoke earlier), but also the sinew and the hide glue. Remember, this is all water soluble. If we were to lay the bow in a tub of water, before too long the glue would dissolve and the threads would all fall off. No good, that!

It's best to figure that, on rainy days, the bow will stay at home. When it rained, the Indians went home. And that's just about the truth. The bow was no good in wet weather. Even if it wasn't sinew backed, the strings, which were made mostly of sinew or rawhide, would be worthless.

The most common method of protecting the sinewed bow in days of old was to coat it liberally with grease, with some brains maybe thrown in for good measure. The smell? Well, I don't do mine that way.

I have coated some with a spar varnish, which didn't seem to hurt the sinew at all, but I just didn't like the brand-new shiny look of a factory-made bow on my completely hand-made primitive piece. I now coat all my bows liberally with a paste wax. This coats both the wood and the sinew, and lets me control the finish.

I've read in one source of intestines being used to cover the bow for protection. In two sources I've seen discussions of skins of serpents (notably rattlesnakes) being used for the same thing.

I have looked hard at old bows all my life, whenever I've come close to them. They fascinate me. Since I began making them, I've looked even more diligently, often taking notes and photographs. In the last coupla years I've examined well over 100 original bows. This includes the bows on display at the Smithsonian Institution in Washington, D.C.; the Museum of the Plains Indians in Cody, Wyoming; and museums and National Historic Sites too numerous to mention. Of all the bows I've seen, probably about half of them were sinew backed, and *not one of them* had either intestine or snakeskin covering. And that figure does not include the Smithsonian report of 1893 by Otis Mason on bows, arrows, and quivers; of the 43 bows illustrated, most were sinew backed, but not one was covered.

These coverings *do* work. They're just not museum quality. I personally like the neat lines of the sinew backing, and I don't like to cover what is, to me, a part of the beauty and labor of my hand-made bow.

String

It's about time now, I guess, to make a string for the bow.

The best natural material to use here, which is what the Indians thought also, is sinew or rawhide. Most vegetable fibers aren't strong enough for this task, though some will work for lighter-weight bows.

I was once informed by two different people that one of the better bowstrings could be made from the neck skin of a large turtle. I was told that, unlike sinew or rawhide, this won't stretch when wet. Find a turtle, "case skin" (like pulling a sock inside out) its neck, and cut the cord spirally (like a barber pole), then stretch it and allow it to dry. This now is all that I can tell you about it, as I've never seen one nor tried it myself—yet.

Deer rawhide makes for a good, strong, long-lasting string. Cut it in a strip about 1/4" wide from a circle of good solid rawhide. Begin cutting around the outside of this circle and continue till you get to the center. A surprisingly small piece will give a lot of lace. Then soak the cut lacing till it's pliable, double it and twist it tightly, and stretch it out to let it dry. For heavier bows I'll prepare the lace the same, but then I will "cord" it, making for an even stronger string. Again, do this while it's wet and stretch it to dry. Remember, the finished string will only be as strong as the weakest spot therein, so avoid thin spots and "scores."

Sinew was probably the favorite bowstring of old. Not only was it strong, but also, because of its slightly elastic characteristic, sinew gave an additional snap to the arrow as it was released. So use the leftover threads from backing your bow, or prepare them specifically for this. It's important to keep the threads as close to the same size as possible. One end of the thread will be thicker than the other, so alternate as you splice in, to keep the finished product even. I begin cording with two threads, staggered so that the ends don't meet. You don't want the splices to adjoin, as this will weaken the whole. Threads should also be soaked to make the cording process easier.

Double this "two-ply" and begin cording. Kink the thread, not evenly in half, between the thumb and forefinger of the left hand (for right-handers), twist the individual two-ply strands tightly in one direction, and then twist this in the other direction over the other individual two-ply strand. (This sounds confusing as all hell, but read it slowly and carefully, and you should be able to follow it.) Thus your two-ply will become a four-ply cord. (Cording is covered extensively in Chapter 1.) Splice in threads as you proceed. Many small splices make for a stronger string.

Arrow

Up to this point, you might have done everything perfectly, but, if the arrow isn't made properly, it won't fly true. Then you might as well sharpen the end of the bow and use it as a spear. Yes, everything said so far is important, but if anything is to be considered all-important here, it would be the arrow. If it won't fly consistently to where you want it, it's worthless. Therefore, much care should be spent in the manufacture thereof.

Here again I'll stress that this is the way that I make *my* arrows. Not only do they work, but they're museum-quality, Plains Indians arrows. I take a few extra steps here that aren't necessary for you to end up with good-quality shooters, and I'll tell you which ones you can skip over and still end up with a suitable product. I'll also stick in, wherever suitable, other methods of ending up with the same. *I spend from 10 to 12 hours making each arrow.*

The materials that can be used for the shaft are many. The main requirements are that it be strong enough to sustain the force of the bow shooting it, and that it be straight. Any 3/8" to 5/8" limb, bush, or shoot is a possible candidate. Something as flimsy as *cattail* stems can even be used. In the southern parts of this country, reeds have been used extensively. As with any other project, the Indians of old used what was available to them. Although I have quite a variety of materials to choose from here in Kansas (*willow, chokecherry, ash cedar,* and more, some of which I could cut into lengths and then split arrow shafts from them), I favor working with *dogwood.* It's abundant and makes up into real nice arrows. These I also cut in the dead of winter while the sap's down.

When cutting them, I look for shafts that are as straight and as knot free as possible. Extra time spent now in the selecting will more than pay for itself later on. For my shafts, I like them to be approximately 3/8" thick when I cut them. I finish mine out at 1/4" and, by the time I remove the bark from them, they're just about right. If they're too thick, then I have to spend extra time removing wood down to size.

I bundle and tie the shafts in groups of 15 or so and hang them in the house to dry. Tying keeps them from warping too severely. In two to four weeks, they're ready to work.

*Bundle of shafts (**left**) and chosen shaft lying next to a finished arrow (**right**).*

Arrowmaking tools: sanding block, knife, bone sizer/wrench, and jawbone for straightening wrench once arrow is finished.

Once you've got the cured shafts, the basic steps to a finished arrow are:

1. Scraping and sizing
2. Preliminary straightening
3. Sanding
4. Cutting of notches
5. More straightening
6.* Cutting of lightning grooves
7. Attaching of point
8. Straightening again
9.* Cresting (painting an owner's mark)
10. Fletching (put feathers on)
11. Sealing

* You can skip these steps.

As you can see, there's lots of straightening to be done. With primitive arrows, straightening is something that you'll be doing over and over, for the life of the arrow.

The first thing to do is to study the shaft, determine the length of the finished arrow, and place this within the shaft. All my shafts have knots. Wherever a leaf has grown there'll be a knot, a site that will always tend to warp. If possible, I try to place the arrow *where no knot will be in the areas that will have feathers of sinew ties* (though this isn't always possible). Knots are prone to future warping, and you won't be able to heat the area to restraighten it if it's been covered. So it helps to watch the placement thereof. Once this is determined, I cut the shaft to length. I don't worry about which end is point or nock, since I'll work the entire length to the same size anyhow.

Using the edge of a sharp knife or a piece of flint, begin scraping the shaft, starting at the point end. Work an area about 4" to 6" long, constantly turning the shaft as you work. When I'm able to run the bone sizer up the shaft, I'll work up another coupla inches or so till I finally reach the nock end. I like the sizer to fit loosely over the shaft, because when the shaft is heated to straighten it will swell slightly. I use the same tool for straightening.

*Scraping shaft (**top left**), sizing shaft (**top right**), carefully shaving any high knots (**above**).*

As I approach the nock end of the arrow, I cut around the shaft and leave the last 1/4" or so of the shaft the original size, sometimes leaving the bark on. This, done in a variety of ways, was common to many of the arrows of old. For the most part, the American Indian didn't use the Mediterranean (white man's) style of release, but actually pinched the nock of the arrow between thumb and forefinger and so needed something to grip. This style of release also strengthens the arrow at this point against the force of the string.

To look down the shaft now, you'll see that it ain't as straight as it might be; it has lots of bumps, bends, and cricks. Really, it's not too pretty, but it'll get better—and soon.

We now will heat and straighten the shaft, using the same bone tool that was used in sizing. The identical process for heating the bow applies here: slowly and carefully. The slightest scorch here will tell, and when the arrow hits something solid it will break. I normally work three or more arrows at a time so that when I heat and straighten one, it cools while I work on the others, and it's cooled enough by the time I get back to it that I don't have to worry about rebending areas that I've already worked. (Got that?) Take your time. Get the arrow as straight as you can. With some of the poorer shafts, this may take some doing, but stick with it. The bumps of knots will look like hell right now, but just kinda look "through" them and get the main part of the shaft straight. Remember to keep lots of grease on the shaft to guard against scorching. It will only take a minute or so to get the shaft hot enough to bend.

Once you've got the arrow straight, or as straight as you can get it, you can (or not, as you wish), wash the grease off with hot water and detergent. This is only to prevent it from building up in the sandstone or paper in the next step. Normally I don't wash it off.

Before, sanding with block, and after.

This next step, sanding, will do wonders for your cricked shaft. Using two pieces of sandstone about 5" to 6" long with a groove cut for the shaft—or with a 2" x 2" block of wood the same length, cut in half lengthwise, and with the grooves cut for the shaft, *and using sandpaper*—place the shaft in the groove and run it several times through this. Almost magically, the "cricked" stick will take on the appearance of a lathe-turned dowel. The length of the shaft-smoother cuts the high spots of knots and other bad spots, leaving the lower parts untouched. After you repeat this several times, brushing the stone or paper in between to keep it clean, you'll find that the shaft has been wonderfully transformed.

Now return to the fire and grease or heat, and straighten again. You should end up with a fine-looking shaft.

Many of the "old" arrows had grooves cut from the base of the feathers to the point, sometimes two but more commonly three. These were just slight cuts made lengthwise along the shaft with knife, stone, or bone. Sometimes they were straight, sometimes wavy, sometimes with zigzags or any combination thereof. The true purpose of these cuts has been lost. Some refer to them as blood grooves, others as lightning grooves. Whatever, if you want them, now's the time to put them in.

Cutting the groove to fit the arrowhead can require a number of approaches. In some situations, you may just want to sharpen and fire harden the tip. (I always think of fire hardening as removing only whatever moisture remains in the wood.) Or you may want to splice in a blunt tip, which is easily enough done, to make an arrow that's deadly on small game. But for large game, we'll want a more appropriate "cutting" point. Bone or stone may be used (the preparation thereof is covered in Chapter 2), in which case, especially for the stone point, some custom sawing or fitting will be in order. I use either a hacksaw or, just as often, a serrated piece of flint, to saw into the tip of the shaft. This, in conjunction with a *sharp* knife, can snug an awkward piece in little time.

Most commonly, though, because of modern game laws, metal points will be used. About any sheet metal will make a serviceable point—including scrap metal, part of an old fender, or, as I commonly use, a barrel hoop. A hacksaw and a file will give you a point of your choosing.

The resulting metal points can usually be mounted snugly within a saw cut.

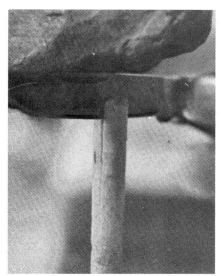 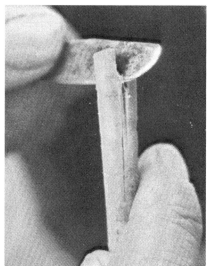

The more common approach in a primitive situation would be to carefully split the shaft for 1" or so up the middle, and then to cut the sides to fit the point. Securing the point with glue and sinew will reinforce the split.

Whatever the type of point or method of cutting, I always seat the point with hide glue, which dries harder than wood and really reinforces. I finish it all off with a good wrapping of sinew. Pine pitch can be used for glue, or none at all. And instead of sinew, nature offers vegetable fibers galore that would suffice.

Now also cut the nock for the string. You'll see from the photos how I do mine. No special advice needed here, just fit the string.

I have read in two accounts that the Indians cut the notch for the string parallel to the arrowhead for hunting purposes and at 90 degrees from it for war purposes. This was supposedly to allow the arrowhead to slide more readily between the ribs of whatever game they were after. I personally think that this is a lot of bunk, since the arrow, as soon as it leaves the string, is spinning, if ever so slightly. But I do make mine to conform to "hunting" style.

Now's a good time to wash the arrow to remove any oils or grease, especially where the feathers will be applied.

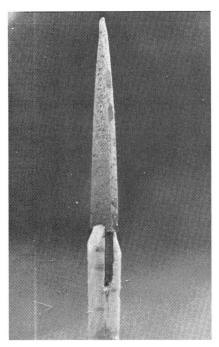
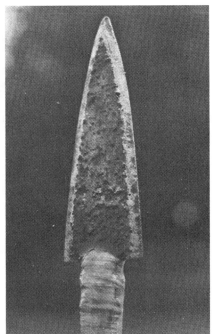

If so desired, now's also the time to paint, or crest, the arrow. In days gone by, this was done to show who belonged to the meat—or scalp. Sort of the owner's signature.

Fletching means applying feathers to stabilize the arrow in flight. This can be a real pain, but is pretty much a necessity. A simple method, shown to me by an arrow maker and flintknapper, was to simply tie two feathers, one on either side of the shaft, at the point end, allowing the back end to lie alongside the shaft. Although I haven't done this myself, I've seen it work, very well. In a primitive situation, this would be just the ticket.

I do things a bit more complicated. I generally work with wild turkey feathers, using the tail feathers if I have them, wing feathers otherwise. Choose three feathers all having the same bend (same wing or same side of the tail). Three feathers will make two arrows.

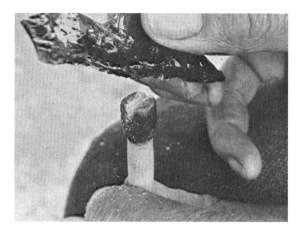

Sawing of notch in nock with serrated obsidian.

To prepare, gently pound the quill portion down the entire length of the feather, which will allow it to split more readily. Then using a knife, or a bone or stone tool, split it evenly the entire length. All one side of the feathers for one arrow, the other side for another. We're trying to keep everything as equal as possible.

Two smaller goose feathers, secured only at bottom.

Now cut the feathers of one arrow to the same length. Mine are made between 5" and 6" inches long, though this length isn't really necessary. Make whatever length you like. Trim the vane up at both ends for about 1/2" for tying to the shaft, and also trim the entire feather vane to about 3/8"—actually, the longer the feather, the narrower the vane. Use a sharp knife to trim the bottom of the quill (the part to fit to the shaft) so that the feather will lie flat. If it has any tendency to curl in one direction, cut through the quill *only on the inside of the curl* wherever necessary. Just get it to lie flat, with the vanes pointed up. Finish off by sanding the bottom of the quill smooth. Some people remove the pith of the quill; I don't. Finally, taper and smash the lower portion of the quill so that when it leaves the bow it will run smoothly over your hand and the bow.

Carefully splitting feather.

Now comes the "funnest" part: attaching the damn things to the shaft in some semblance of order. It can try the patience of most, especially me.

One vane will be applied at a 90° angle to the notch of the nock, the other two vanes placed at equal distances from that. This allows the two "bottom" feathers to run smoothly over the bow. Most folks color the upper vane differently so as to be able to place it in the string more quickly. The majority of "old" arrows weren't colored that way, so I don't do it. Begin by running a sinew thread, wetted, around the shaft about 1/2" below the nock, tying down the first "up" feather. Then, with additional revolutions around the shaft, tie down the other two. Pull and push the feathers with your fingernails so that they're in proper position, then wrap them tight. Finish by sealing the thread with a drop or two of hide glue to hold it all in place.

When this has been accomplished, begin again with the "up" feather at the other end. Pull that smooth against the shaft and begin wrapping with another sinew thread. Here, unlike the upper tie, don't let the sinew thread run *under* any of the feathers. Remember that this is the end that will have to run "into" your hand and the bow as it's released. The smoother that this is kept, the better. So tie all three of the feathers at the same time, wrap a few times with the thread, but before you get it too tight, use your fingernails to rotate the feathers so that they lie straight with the shaft. Take a coupla more tighter wraps, and then "bite" the edge of your knife into the end of the quill and pull on it ever so gently so as to pull the vane tight. It'll then lie pretty much flat on the shaft. If you pull too hard, it's possible to pull the upper end out from its tie.

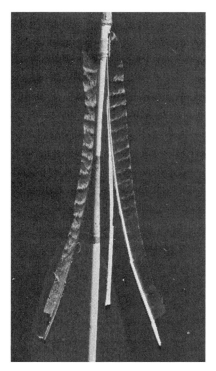

*Fletching tied at top (**above**); tied top and bottom (**right**).*

The arrow should now look like an arrow—soooooo pretty! If done as I've described, it'll be museum quality. It's now ready to use, but here's a historical note: I believe that about half the arrows of old had the feathers being left as is, and half had feathers glued down. Myself, I prefer to glue them down. So if that's what you want, melt down a small batch of hide glue in *hot* water (just a bit of water here). It's best if the glue sets up fast, the thicker the better. With a pointed stick, apply a bead of glue to each side of the feathers. If they bow away from the shaft a bit, they can be held in gently with the fingers till the glue sets.

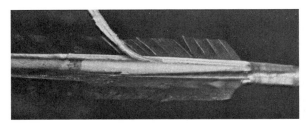

Gluing down of fletching.

Top view of fletching.

When all the glues have set up well, in just a coupla hours, it's wise to go over the entire shaft with a paste wax. I'd use wax in lieu of a varnish, because you'll more than likely have to reheat and straighten the shaft in the future.

What has just been described makes for a damn fine arrow. You can make an equally serviceable one by *not* adding all the little touches that make this a museum-quality piece. In a truly primitive situation, I certainly wouldn't worry myself with lightning grooves, cresting, fancily applied feathers, or perfectly sized shafts. I *would* concentrate on a "true" shaft, so that it would fly straight; have a point of sorts, nothing fancy (you only need to penetrate the chest cavity of any critter and it'll be dead, and even a sharpened stick would do that); and have some sort of fletching. Any feather would work, even a strip of carefully crafted bark.

Our finished arrow with two others.

*The finished sinew-backed hickory bow, 45" long, tops my 50 lb. scale at 17"— leaving me with probably about an 80 lb. bow with my 22" arrow (**bottom**).*

Top: *Layout of pieces of a "typical hunting" bow case and quiver of the Plains Indians. The lower portion of the quiver is rawhide sewn in with sinew.* **Bottom:** *All together.*

Chapter 5

Makin' Meat – 2

The early mountain men of the American West proudly used the phrase "makin' meat" to note that they had obtained sustenance, mostly by having shot some game animal. "This child shore had starvin' times for nigh on ten days afore he made meat," written in a journal, could be interpreted to mean that the diarist had spent 10 days with no nourishment and then had shot something, trapped something, knocked a bird silly with a rock, or even found a half-eaten or rotted carcass left by some wolves.

Obtaining Sustenance in Nature

Deadfalls, Snare, Fish Trap, Atlatl, and More

This chapter delves into various methods of subsisting in the wilderness. Chapter 4 covers how to make a bow and arrow from nature. (Actually, the bow and arrow is quite a ways up the ladder when it comes to primitive gathering.)

After a warning. I'll begin this chapter with a trapline, the first thing that an experienced woodsperson would pursue if or when placed in a primitive situation. On our line you'll note that most of the sets will be for small critters such as mice, rats, rabbits, and birds. This is because it's an initial primitive situation; that is, what you'd be depending on for life, if you found yourself in the wilds with no lunch. Small things will keep you going. Large critters will be a bonus. We'll also set a coupla fish-type traps.

HANTAVIRUS
Pulmonary Syndrome

When it comes to any study of primitive living skills, trapping is a necessary subject. We firmly believe that trapping was, and is, responsible for the majority of sustenance in any sort of survival or primitive living effort.

Plants can be gathered in everyday movements with minimal effort, in many cases, but also with a minimal return of essential nutrients and calories (as noted in several other places in this book). Time spent hunting, in our opinion, is time better spent on other living projects, using the hunting tools for opportunistic moments.

Traps will catch and hold just about any form of animal life, from fish to insects to deer-sized game, but by far the major source of sustenance will come from small, rodent-sized animals. Consuming all or most parts of these quarry will supply most or all of the nutrients and calories necessary for the human body not only to survive but to thrive.

Since 1993, however, there have been 465 confirmed instances in the United States of a viral disease, *hantavirus pulmonary syndrome* (HPS), which has a very high mortality rate. The host for this virus? Rodents.

The first reports came from the Four Corners area of the Southwest. Several persons on the Navajo Indian Reservation died suddenly. It seems that many of the infected people had been collecting piñon nuts (seeds), which had been conveniently stored for them in caches by rodents, most notably deer mice. There had been a hearty crop of the piñon nut, which led to a heavier than normal population of deer mice, caused, some theorize, by unseasonably heavy rains. Whatever, the deer mouse was pinpointed as the source.

Since then, there have been cases of HPS reported in 30 states: all of the West, parts of the Southeast into Florida, up into the Northeast into New York and Rhode Island, and even into Canada. Three fourths of the cases have been from rural areas.

Hey folks, that's like saying that the entire country has it.

Various hantaviruses are known throughout the world (the name comes from a river in Korea), and there are several distinct viruses (or species). Those (un)lucky enough to contract it in Europe have only a 1 percent chance of dying, while in Asia this is upped to 15 percent. The strains in the Americas are much more lethal. When first reported, the mortality was a whopping 70 percent, but has since dropped to about 35 percent, probably because of better communication and awareness among medical personnel. The higher fatality rate comes from the fact that in the American strain (HPS), the lungs rapidly fill with fluid.

The range of the primary carrier, the deer mouse, covers most all of the U.S. And tests on them have shown the virus to exist throughout most of its range. Other carriers are the cotton rat (Florida), rice rat (Southeast), white-footed mouse (Northeast), the so-called piñon mouse, and the western chipmunk. A carrier of the not-so-dangerous Seoul virus (distributed worldwide) is the Norway rat. The infected rodents exhibit no visible symptoms. The list, both of viruses and of carriers, has expanded since 1993. Human cases of HPS have been positively identified in the U.S. as early as 1978 and inferred back to 1959.

In all cases to date, victims were infected by coming into contact with the feces, urine, or saliva of infected rodents. Since the virus is in the body fluids, it can be assumed that it is throughout the body. Most cases reportedly were a result of *breathing the dust* of disturbed feces, saliva, or urine of infected rodents.

If your hands come in contact with anything that's contaminated and then reach your mouth or nose, there's a chance of infection.

The survival time in the environment is unknown. Periods of up to two days on a dried surface are suggested. You can also get the virus by being bitten by an infected rodent. So far there's no evidence that it can be transmitted from person to person or from insects (such as fleas).

The virus is easily killed with most general-purpose household disinfectants (bleach, alcohol). In other words, if you got a lot of nests or feces in your woodpile, shed, or outhouse, it would be best to spray it down with a disinfectant prior to cleaning it up. A 1 percent (1:100) dilution of household bleach is suggested for wiping down potentially contaminated surfaces. A more concentrated dilution of 10 percent is suggested for heavily contaminated areas such as nest sites. A fresh solution should be mixed daily.

Just how concerned should you be? Well, of deer mice tested in three counties of western Kansas in 1993, 9 percent were infected. We live in north central Kansas, so that's getting pretty close to home.

You don't have to stick your head in a bucket of mouse scat and take a deep breath to become infected. One sniff is all it takes.

Something as mundane as moving the woodpile, with the accompanying mice and packrat nests, becomes hazardous. A little mathematics: Using 9 percent as the baseline, if there's one mouse nest in the pile, there's a 9 percent chance that it's infected. Two nests, 18 percent. If among all the wood we move around here there are nine nests, there's a 100 percent chance that we'll come into contact with HPS. If infected, there's a 50 percent chance of dying from it. That doesn't sound like good odds to me.

For clean-up of rodent contaminated areas, the Centers for Disease Control and Prevention (CDC) recommends the complete wetting down of the area with a disinfectant, wearing of an approved respirator (in enclosed spaces with heavy, active rodent infestations), wearing of rubber gloves, washing of the rubber gloves with a disinfectant when finished, followed by the washing of your hands and burying or burning of any suspected materials. Whew!

Symptoms are flu-like: fever; muscle aches; abdominal, joint, and lower back pain; headaches; cough; nausea; vomiting; and diarrhea. If any of these symptoms are exhibited, in a period up to six weeks after possible exposure, seek help immediately!

Since there's no known curative drug, prompt medical attention is a MUST to increase the chances of survival.

How does this affect us primitives? Let me tell you that Geri and I don't mess with mice and packrats very much anymore. Recommended precautions for campers and hikers, besides the obvious steps of avoiding contact with nests or burrows, include not sleeping directly on the ground—though, for us, that's as natural as making cordage. Mice pee everywhere they go, leaving a scent trail, so sleeping on the ground increases the risks of your breathing this.

This is serious business. One touch or sniff and you're in trouble.

And yet...trapping, like friction firemaking, ranks right up there at the top of the primitive's priority list. Can we discontinue this practice? Should we?

We still teach and write about the importance of traps, and also how, in a real survival or primitive situation, we may have to depend on some rodents. We have to. Primitive living and survival demand this knowledge. In a survival situation, the risks must be weighed. True, the human body can go several weeks without any food at all. But we stress staying away from the mice and other listed carriers if, and when, possible. Each individual has to make his or her own decisions.

Knowledge, awareness, caution, and weighing of the facts of the personal risks by each individual are in order.

The list of concerns grows constantly. What was considered safe yesterday just might not be today, or tomorrow.

Suspect all rodents. Put off limits those that are, for sure, hosts of this deadly virus. Packrats, and wood rats, are not on the list—yet. So what do you do if you catch one? Or a squirrel? A muskrat? Weigh the facts and the situation.

Heat kills. HPS is a fragile virus. If all portions of the rodent are subjected to a high-enough temperature, the disease is killed. The safest way that we've come up with to handle this would be to, first, not handle with the hands. Shove a stick in its mouth or butt, and be careful of any blood or other fluids. Singe the hair off, scrape with another stick (burn the sticks, trying not to inhale the smoke), and place the critter directly in the coals. Or boil it. Or roast in a makeshift oven. Fry it on a flat hot rock. Whatever you do, don't handle the animal until it's been well cooked, meaning until the meat isn't pink and even then-some. It should reach 140°F (better yet, 160°) for at least 20 minutes. (This message comes to us direct from the CDC.)

Carrying the suspect animal in a basket will require the burning of the basket. The danger lies not so much in the cooking and eating as in the earlier handling. A rock or log falling on an animal is enough to literally squeeze the pee outta him, and breathing the fumes can infect you. Use caution!

The above was written by me in 1996 and updated for this book. I wish to acknowledge Michael H. Bradshaw and Liz Boyle, Extension Specialists at Kansas State University, and Lori Miller and Kristi Busico, of the Centers for Disease Control in Atlanta, for their help in obtaining information contained in this chapter. When I first contacted them, they were kinda at a loss for answers pertaining to HPS and the eating of mice. It just wasn't one of the areas that they study. The information presented here was gathered with their help.

A fact sheet (MF-1117) can be obtained from the Cooperative Extension Service, Kansas State University, Manhattan, KS 66531. Information can also be obtained by calling the CDC in Atlanta at 800-532-9929 or writing the Department of Health and Human Services, Public Health Service, CDC, Atlanta, GA 30333.

Some or all of the trap types that I will show are illegal in many states (possibly most). Check your local regulations. Also, one of the trigger mechanisms I'll discuss can easily be set to hurt, maim, or even kill large game, including the human species.

What I'll show is how you can subsist in a truly primitive or survival situation. I'll explain how and where to place some of the sets so as to possibly catch some of the larger species of game, from which (besides just nourishment) you could derive furs, skins, sinew, and bones (dealt with in other chapters). Some of the traps, if left set around your home or grounds, could be detrimental to the well-being of your neighbors' cats, dogs, or children. ***Use caution!***

One big thing here is to think small. Mice, packrats, minnows, crawdads, insects—all will sustain life. If you were to approach your primitive situation thinking only of larger game, you might starve.

Something else to think about: You could eat only the meat of wild game for weeks on end, and starve anyway! Wild game isn't marbled with fat, unlike our usual diet of domesticated meat. Creatures in the wild are running around for their very lives, and don't build up large stores of fat.

You may have to break prejudices of eating habits that you have. In a primitive situation, especially if it's a case of survival, you may have no choice what goes through your mouth. Basically, the hair and skin and intestines will go out, the rest will go in, except larger bones (you'll roast or boil the larger bones and remove the succulent marrow). Cooking methods are given in Chapter 7.

A story that I read somewhere: During the last century a ship was ice locked in the Arctic and the crew taken in by the natives. Come spring, all but one (or two) were dead and the authorities at first thought that the Inuits had murdered them, till it came to light that the white man ate only the red meat, whereas the natives ate almost the entire animal. Stomach contents and the marrow of the bone didn't appeal to the whites, so they fastidiously starved to death with full stomachs. Something else for you to be thinking about before taking to the wilds.

Various plants can make up much of the diet, but I can't go into that as my knowledge on this is extremely limited. There are many guides on the market to fill your appetite for edible plants.

Once there's enough meat on hand in your camp, I'll show you the old, natural way of preserving it. Do remember, though, that if you get bad meat, bad tallow, or bad berries, I assume no responsibility for…bad bellies.

The Trap Line

One thing that just about all outdoorsmen, woodsmen, and survivalists will agree on is the fact that the trap line is the *most* expedient method of keeping a supply of meat on hand with a minimum of effort.

If, for some reason, you're on the move, a couple (or several) traps might be set out each night. But if you're in a good area that supplies all your needs (food source, water, and shelter) and decide to spend some time in one location, then there you'd set out one or more "lines." By line, I mean a certain number of traps set in any given location—up a certain creek, or along a certain ridge, or south of camp or north of camp, and so on.

I'll only mention a few tips that apply to trapping. It's a profession in itself, and there are numerous books on the market to teach you the art of trapping any particular type of critter that you decide to specialize in. The same with hunting techniques. I can't begin to impart to you all the knowledge necessary to become one with nature—that's up to you. Instead, I'll give you the tools and information necessary to begin. It's up to you to apply them, but you'll have to be aware that you can't catch it if it ain't there—so look for *fresh* signs and then trap or hunt accordingly.

Also, here, with the deadfall and snare, I'll show you one *trigger system* (actually, now three of them). There are several that are shown, and shown, and shown in survival-type and outdoors books. I've tried a few of them. *None* works to the satisfaction that I desire, and most are, I believe, only perpetuated myths. They look good on paper and sometimes seem to work—and so are included in any or all books dealing with this subject.

I thought for a long time about how I could get a 80 to 100 lb. rock to fall where I wanted it to and when it was supposed to, *nearly 100 percent of the time*. And yet have it be simple enough to set that the entire time, from making the trigger to the finished set, took only a few minutes. I spent one year showing the trigger system that I came up with to any and all outdoorsmen that I came across. No one has yet been able to say that they knew of it, and all agreed that it does work.

So pay attention to the accompanying photos and what I say, then go out to your backyard and make it work. My first set, from the initial inspiration to completed working deadfall with a 123 lb. rock, took right at 20 minutes. Your first should take no more time than this.

To make this work, you'll need about 12" to 15" of cordage (see Chapter 1 for details).

You'll see from the photos that the trigger needs to be shaved down somewhat at one end, to hold it in the knot of cordage on the other piece of the trigger.

Well, hell, I'm not even gonna try to describe this system in words. Instead, I'll just insert photos and write captions for them. Actually, some photos won't even need words.

My trigger system—so simple, so easy to construct in a primitive wilderness situation, and so effective.

The most efficient part of this trigger is that it's set before you position your 100 lb.-plus rock— in this case, 123 lb.

The baited, set trigger. A scrap of meat is held to it by cordage. The trigger fits into the cordage tied around the stick driven into the ground. Round on round. The slightest "busying" of the bait will release it all.

Note that a separate piece of cordage is tied to the weight-holding stick, to pull it when the spring releases. Initially I used the spring stick to push the upright out, but here the spring is less likely to push away your supper along with the stick. Always remember to use dead or dry sticks for the spring sticks. Green ones will conform to the bend and lose their spring.

Left: Deadfall set near packrat house. Upper right: Three mornings later, the tripped trap. Lower right: Bingo—meat!

Left: *Deadfall set for packrat. The baited trigger is placed on the left side of the underside of the rock, and the left side is blocked by another upright rock so that when the trap is triggered, the animal must travel farther to escape.*

Right: *Three mornings later...meat! And, yes, this packrat we ate.*

The same trigger system set as a snare. Bait is on the trigger, noose is on the ground. Many, many applications for this.

Woodland trail set snare—can you spot it?

Left: *Trail set snare; note trigger.* **Right:** *Trail kinda blocked, to help guide the critter through the noose. Of the three mornings that I had this set, it was tripped once, with the noose drawn up but no evidence of any critter. The other two mornings, the noose had been disturbed by passing animals. The noose needs to be just the right size—too large, and animals will run through it; too small, they'll only push it aside.*

Top: *Stout snare set at pond. Snares (three of them) were set out on the ground from baited trigger. Here it's better to use triggers of about 1" diameter rather than the illustrated 1/4".* **Bottom:** *Geri hauling in drowned possum.*

In my morning's mail some years back was an envelope from Steve Watts, a primitive-skills instructor for the Schiele Museum of Natural History in Gastonia, North Carolina. Quoting his note: "John: Hope all is well with you. I just ran across this deadfall trigger (a new one to me). It's like greased lightning. Got it from Henry Rhyne (a local old-time trapper). Henry says that he got it from a trapper in Alaska in the 1940s. Says it was mostly used for birds. You might already know it, but as I say, it was a new one on me. Take care—Keep it up. Steve."

Well, Steve, and folks, it's also a new one for me, and it *does* work. Of all my inquiring about deadfall triggers, and of all the folks that I ran into when I was preparing this chapter, this is one that works. Steve's initial response to my inquiry was that he knew only the old standbys (which I don't mention here, because of the percentage of failures). So now you have another *good,* usable trigger. Where this would come in the handiest is on hard surfaces where driving the second trigger piece into the ground would be out of the question. The drawback would be the careful carving necessary on hardwood.

The four views of the trigger sent me by Steve Watts should be self-explanatory. Bait is placed under a rock or a "live box" (meant to capture a critter alive, rather than killing it). The slightest downward pressure to the stick releases it all—as Steve says, "like greased lightning." Bait can be placed on end of stick or ground, as birds will perch on it to eat.

Geri and I went once to a weeklong "Cave Man's Convention" in central Oregon, hosted by Jim Riggs and Brian James. What a great sharing of primitive skills that mostly, but far from all, dealt with flintknapping. One of the other tips gleaned was Jim's old standby, the Paiute deadfall trigger system. This does work, but with much difficulty when setting heavy falls for large game. (The same applies to the second trigger sent by Steve.) But when setting out *many* traps in your line, you can't know too many triggers. Where one might be just the checker for a particular set, another might not be at all usable. Pick and choose what works best for your situation as it arises.

Looky—another goodie from Jim Riggs, a Paiute deadfall trigger. **Top:** *Jim checking out my work.* **Bottom:** *Front view. Study the two photos carefully, as they show all that's needed to construct your own. The upright and horizontal trigger pieces and the cordage are all the same length. The short piece tied (or through a loop) to cordage needs to be stiff. The lower thin piece going from that to the bottom of the rock could be a stout stem of grass, as little force will be applied to it. Bait is placed where the thin stick (or stem of grass) touches the rock. Jim's only comment about my setting of this was that the upright* shouldn't *be under the rock, just in case the horizontal fails to kick it free. When touched at bait, though, the rock fell as it was designed to. Also, not visible but very important is the slight groove cut into the top of the upright to hold the horizontal.*

I've always believed in the power of photographs, but with these traps we've had some questions posed as to their construction, so we're now including line drawings of three of them to help clarify.

The only change you'll note is with the construction of the Paiute deadfall. This trigger I've always touted as the easiest and fastest to make, but the hardest and most time-consuming to set, so we seldom, if ever, used it. But exasperation finally got me to experimenting. Two changes, and our trapping world turned over! Now this trap is what we use for our bread and butter. It's fast and easy not only to construct but *now* also to set. With basic instructions, we've had 10- and 12-year-olds setting them in mere minutes. And it *has* been proven in the field.

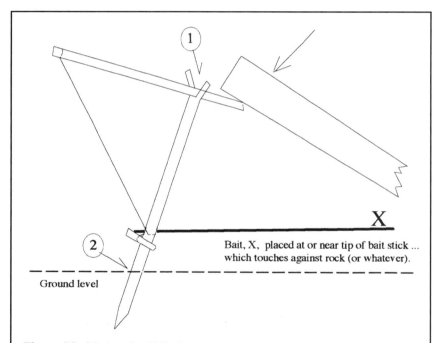

Bait, X, placed at or near tip of bait stick ... which touches against rock (or whatever).

Ground level

The modified Paiute deadfall trigger. two major changes, both in the upright stick. 1) Use of a natural "Y" to support the horizontal piece and 2) pushing the upright into the ground to stabilize it ... this being the most critical change. Just insure that the upright is far enough out to prevent the weight from falling onto it or even brushing against it which will slow it down. For most efficiency, keep the two wood pieces at approx. 90° angle - which will keep the string at approx. 45°.

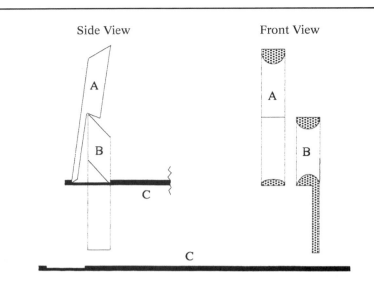

Side View

Front View

A

B

C

C

A

B

This trap is slick but much time is required in making it - a hard wood is more effective because the four contact points will round easily if made from softer woods ... and once rounded, it becomes a real trick to set.

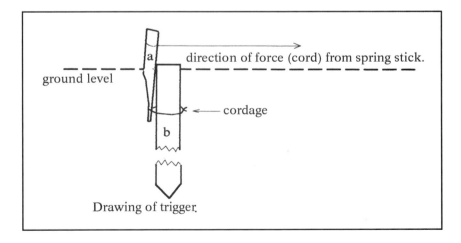

direction of force (cord) from spring stick.

ground level

a

cordage

b

Drawing of trigger.

The following trap was shown to us by Gordon Nagorski of Ontario, Canada.

*The basic setup as shown (**left**) from the front quarter and from (**right**) the side. This is a good set, so the front will be the entrance.*

Left: *A close-up of the trigger.*
Right: *The other end of the trigger.*

Left: *The setup (before making "step" on bottom stick or trigger). Study closely how this is put together, referring back to the close-up of the upper part of the trigger. A single piece of cordage is looped around the deadfall log and over, very near the rounded tip, of the trigger. The bottom of the trigger is held by a stick going crosswise between the slanted pieces stuck into the ground (and tied at the top).*
A cord is run from the cross stick to the step stick (bottom trigger), tying it above the ground so that stepping on it pulls the top cross out, thus releasing the upper trigger and killing log.

Left: *Sticks placed on bottom trigger to form step.*

Right: *Bark placed over that for reinforcement and firmness.*

The set made into a cubby. Bait is placed beyond the "step." Two smaller logs can be placed at the front so that the deadfall log will fall between, thereby (you hope) breaking the back of the trapped critter. Distance from where the "dead falls" (ha, gotcha there!) to the step is critical. Remember that the animal's front legs will be on the "step," and place it accordingly so that its midback is under the falling log.

Geri pushes on the step and it all comes tumbling down—fast! Note trigger flying off.

OK, now you've got a working knowledge of three *good, working* trigger systems that are really simple to put together in a primitive situation. Now let's set up a line. Remember, think small. If by chance (in most parts of the country, a good chance) you have a packrat's house in the area, that would be a great place to set as many as six, or even more, sets. Here a family unit might run as many as six to eight critters. Packrats are a reasonably good-sized animal and worthy of your attention. Just look for signs that the house is occupied (fresh tracks, scat) and set wherever is convenient. Rats are inquisitive and won't need anything fancy to attract them to your set. Any scraps from a previous kill will work as bait, or perhaps some grass seed chewed up well (by you) and made into a paste. That'll get you started. We've even had deadfalls tripped by rats chewing through the cordage—maybe lured by the grease residue left by our fingers?

Most of the critters that we're now looking for will leave definite trails in their wake. Rabbits, mice, and that scale of critter will use the same runs time and again. Their trails will be visible to the naked eye in the grass and leaves. These will make good places to set snares, or just off the trails for baited deadfalls and snares.

If the "right" pool of water is available, you can put out a *stout* snare. Most all critters that you're trapping will eat your snare material (if you're using natural fiber cordage), and actually do include it in their daily diet. You need to kill them, or in this case preoccupy them with staying afloat, so that they won't consider turning around and biting your cordage in two. Just give them a chance to drown.

This is one good reason to use *deadfalls* in lieu of snares whenever possible. Even if you were to catch a rabbit by the hind foot and it wasn't able to reach the cordage (which is unlikely), the ruckus that it would make would attract a coyote or fox, and your dinner would be gone come morning. So, a good lesson here: *deadfall* whenever possible.

Here's an idea for catching *big* meat with a snare (of course, you can see just how you could easily construct a deadfall of almost any size, using the first trigger system illustrated). If you've ever spent time around a campfire in the woods, you've surely heard noises just outside of the circle of light, or maybe even seen eyes reflected in the light, or spotted fresh tracks around (and sometimes inside) the perimeter the next morning—signs of coyotes, raccoons, deer, or large cats. A snare on the ground with a trip cord hooked to the trigger or a baited snare set just *might* get you a larger critter tied up long enough for you to grab your club or spear and apply a fatal wound. But *use caution!* Have a torch ready, or some other light source. I'd hate to run blindly into the dark and try to knock a mountain lion or bear, whether a grizzly or a black, on the head with a stick. And also know the legalities involved. You might get away with these tricks in a survival situation, but on a weekend campout I doubt that your local fish and game commission would turn their heads while you practice your survival skills. Do your practicing on rats and rabbits (if legal in your state).

Set yourself up several lines. Each line might have as many as 50 sets, or as few as 8 or 10. Each situation and locale will be different. Once the lines are in place, it'll take only a glance to check each set, and only a minute or two more to reset if necessary.

All the time that you're in the primitive situation, remember that you'll also be gathering materials for cordage, fire making, bowstaves, arrow shafts, workable stone, bones—anything to make life a little easier in the wilderness.

Now, let's not forget about our feathered friends. I don't know of any birds that you *can't* eat (though you'd better not take my word for that, and maybe do some research on this), but there are some that I would prefer *not* to eat under normal circumstances. I *once* tried coot!

Like birds, rodents are food, protein, something to keep you going. The deadfall trigger sent by Steve Watts, as he mentions, is superb, and probably designed primarily for birds. Our heavier-duty deadfall trigger shown will easily get your crows or raptors (**Caution:** Raptors are protected federally), because meat can be used as a bait, though in most of our sets the bait is hidden from the view of birds.

A net is an ideal way to get all types of birds. The one shown on the following page is very loosely "woven," not "netted," but will catch and hold all birds, as they'll naturally spread their wings when trapped and become further entangled. The net shown is approximately 3 1/2' square and can be triggered by the bird (as shown), or the watching trapper can just let go of the cord and drop it on the birds whenever he has a full-enough house. If you stand by to manually release the net on a given animal, the net is assured relief from a lot of damage if catching a large bird, coon, possum, or coyote. Although the net might hold any of the above (especially a turkey or duck), it wouldn't for very long. Any of these critters would make short work of your net, which will have required many long hours on your part to assemble. If you were to drop it on a bird or birds, or a small critter, a quick run over and a thump on the head with a club (or wringing of their necks) will keep them from damaging the net.

Trigger for the bird net. Notched and will be securely lashed.

Two views showing a set trigger. **Right:** *Note how cordage runs from trigger through crossed stakes, and from there up over tripod and back to net.*

The set bird net. Study closely and follow cordage from trigger, through crossed sticks, over tripod (could be tree limb), and back to top of net.
*The net itself serves as a "spring stick." With just the slightest touch to the trigger, it all came tumbling down (**right**), quick and easy.*

Also as regarding the trap line, let's not forget about fish. If you find yourself close to a water source that supports fish, the use of the impoundment shown will often corral you plenty of nourishment. You can also make a "minnow type" trap out of any straight shoots or limbs.

With some practice, you can teach yourself to be fast enough to catch hold of crawdads as you turn over rocks in river or stream. Their tails are a delicacy. Frogs are not to be forgotten, either.

Also useful, though not really a trap, is the bank line. I've seen drawings of several types of primitive fish hooks, but from personal experience I know just how much a fish will fight, and I know that most of these makeshift hooks of bone or wood, or both, just won't hold up to the strain. One that does work is a straight piece of limber or hard (not brittle) wood or bone, kinda like a rounded toothpick is shaped, with a line tied around the center. This is inserted into a minnow, small frog, insect, or toad and hung from a *limber* stick stuck into the bank. The bait or hook needs to be a little below water level, just slack enough to allow the fish to swallow the bait or hook. Even intestines, scrap meats, or fats can be wrapped around the stick or hook. Fish will swallow this bait, and, once inside their body, the line (since it's tied to the center of the hook) prevents it from being removed or regurgitated. If the cordage is strong enough that the fish's teeth don't wear it through, you've got meat. If you're camped near a water source that will adapt to this, you should put dead leaves and similar materials on the pole to alert you to the fact that there's a fish on, so you can get to it immediately before its teeth cut through your cordage.

 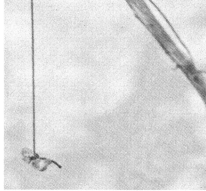

Left: A pair of "gorge" fish hooks, made of green cedar for large catfish (use smaller hooks for smaller fish). ***Right:*** Baited with scrap meat and tied to cordage.

Bankline set (actually, you can barely see a second), with limber poles stuck securely into the bank. Geri is making a fish trap in background.

The same net shown for birds will also catch fish, except here make sure that all weavings of the cordage are tied. (Otherwise, learn to "net"—though that will require more cordage.) The result is a gill net, and it really does work. Fish swim into it and become your supper.

And while you're messing around the water, keep an eye out for freshwater clams. Maybe they're not as tasty as their saltwater cousins, but they did sustain the early Indians. The muddy taste they have can be somewhat relieved by letting them sit in clean, fresh water for several days. My experience with them has left a bit to be desired, but in the primitive state I'm certain that they would improve in flavor considerably.

Well, that basically is what I have to offer on traps. But do remember that the best-made trap set will catch you nothing if it isn't set where the critters are. Learn to look for signs, and set accordingly.

Top: *A fairly simple, yet highly effective, fish trap, placed in the neck of a pond. Any shallow pool in a creek, river, or lake would work, or one set in the riffles between pools of a creek.* ***Bottom:*** *Close-up of how entrance to trap works. Very limber twigs and so on allow fish to enter but prevent their leaving. This set was made without using any cordage, only by interlacing the shoots. Scraps of fats, guts, and so forth are placed within the enclosure, as you hope to draw fish. Check local regulations pertaining to fish traps—this one is illegal in Kansas!*

Gathering

Now we'll go into some techniques for gathering—something that the primitive person will be doing from the moment that he or she becomes primitive. You will *never ever* stop "gathering." Your only tools needed here will be the rabbit stick (also called a throwing or digging stick), a sack or basket, and knowledge of what to gather.

The "rabbit" stick is only a limb or other piece of hardwood, from 18" to 30" long (mine is 27"), heavy enough to go through grass when thrown at rabbits, birds, or whatever, yet light enough to be thrown easily with force. Pointing it at one end will enable you to use it also for digging various roots and tubers. This tool is amazingly effective.

Once you've become accustomed to throwing it accurately, you'll have a fair chance of hitting a critter at up to 100 feet. You may spot a rabbit (look for its eye) before it dashes. It often will run only a few yards and then stop. Often, once you've put a rabbit to flight, a sudden yell or whistle will stop it long enough for you to get a shot. And how often have you almost stepped on a pheasant or a covey of quail before they took to flight? Pheasants in particular seem to hang in midair for several seconds, allowing you a good chance for a hit at 10 to 15 yards. If you miss, though, watch where your stick lands, not the bird, or you'll lose both. If nothing else, a "rabbit rock" will work if you're decent with a baseball. (It has worked for me, and I'm a terrible thrower.)

My personal throwing stick. To make this a rabbit stick, I need only to throw it at a rabbit. It makes quite a whooshing sound as it travels. Thinning it somewhat would help that. From this the boomerang developed. Although a rock would go where this wouldn't, through brush, on open ground, or in the air, this cuts a swath of 27", so I needn't be quite so accurate.

Turn over logs and rocks, and if you're quick enough you'll be able to club surprised mice, rats, or lizards. Be cautious of snakes while doing this, but don't be afraid to club or stone one should it be found. I know of no snake that's not edible (be sure to check this out if unsure). Of course, with rattlesnakes, copperheads, and water moccasins, leave the head alone—as that's where the poison sacs are. The only other poisonous snake in North America is the coral snake, found primarily in the Southeast. I would *not* eat this snake till I learned more about it, as it's a highly venomous snake whose venom affects the nervous system. Fortunately, you normally don't have to worry about being bitten by one because of its small size and mouth.

Making sacks and baskets is covered in Chapter 8, though it really doesn't take much know-how to put together some container in a well-stocked woods, especially with a knowledge of cording (see Chapter 1). A real simple weaving will make a tight-enough sack from almost any cordage material. And limber shoots of willow, dogwood, and similar plants will make a *simple* basket, requiring no special skills or knowledge.

Seeds and *nuts* will be some of your most valuable additions to your diet. You may be wise to check which few aren't edible (such as poison ivy, sumac, or oak), but most are OK. In fact, they're much better than OK. The nutritional value of seeds and nuts is amazing. (Here I'm stepping somewhat out of the realm of my knowledge and into edible plants, so double-check what I say here.) Any grass seed should be welcome. Fruit seeds abound in nature. If in the timber, look for nuts. Acorns can have a bitter tannic removed by leaching several times in water. White oaks have the sweetest acorns (I read that in several places). These all can be ground into a flour, or added to soups and stews as is, and many can be eaten raw. These will be an important addition to your diet.

> **I can't stress enough that you'll have to do your own research on edible plants—not within the scope of this book.**

Here's a tip given to me by a friend who had read it somewhere (take it for what it's worth): Tear apart a packrat's house (only in an emergency, as it *is* his house), maybe after having trapped it as well. The packrat will have stored various seeds and tubers within. Also, its downy beds will make great tinder for making your fire, and will come out dry under the wettest conditions. If you tear apart the packrat house while still occupied, keep your rabbit stick handy. When the packrats first come out, they will be really confused and slow to find shelter or cover. Make meat!

Atlatl

The *atlatl,* or spear-thrower: What a beautiful and efficient tool and weapon, used for thousands of years before the discovery of the bow and arrow. And when you watch someone proficient with this tool, such as two world champions I know, you begin to understand just why the bow was so slow in coming of age.

Distance throws of 70-plus yards are simple with an atlatl. Pie-plate size accuracy at 20 to 30 yards isn't uncommon with practice, plus it's done with all the force necessary to kill large game, such as bison and even mastodon (it's said) in days gone by.

The atlatl (or thrower) itself isn't difficult to construct. (This Aztec word is pronounced roughly *ought-lot-uhl.*) As you can see in the photos, it's nothing more than a cheater, an extension of your arm. Most atlatls average 15" to 20" long. Not only does it extend your arm to create more force, it also takes that force and concentrates it at the *end* of the spear or dart, not in the middle (as in the case of a hand-thrown one). The spear actually bends from the force of the atlatl, thereby creating an additional force as the dart snaps away. And if the atlatl is fine-tuned to the weight of the dart or spear that it's throwing, it will also have a light pliability to it that will "snap" in tune with the dart or spear, in turn producing even more speed and force.

As with the arrow, you'll spend more time making a spear or dart (I'll refer to it as the dart from here on out). The darts run from 4' to 7' in length, with 5' to 6' being the more common length. Much time will be spent in straightening it, as with the arrow (refer to Chapter 4).

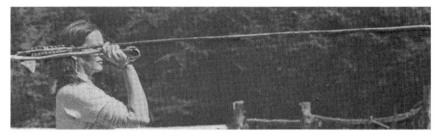

Geri preparing to drop a mastodon with an atlatl.

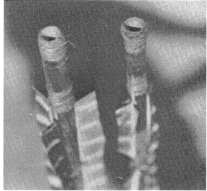

Left: The fuller fletching slowed darts considerably, and trimming helped a lot.
Right: Close-up showing indents for nub to fit into.

Showing how atlatl mates with dart. This could be done just the opposite, with a round tip on the dart and a depression on the atlatl for it to fit into.

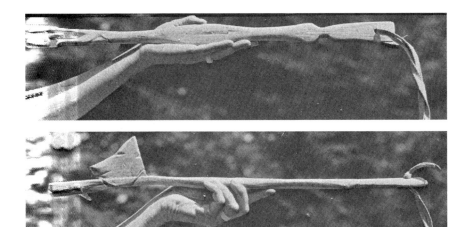

Front and side views of my atlatl. The weight is to counterbalance the weight and length of my darts, but I got a bit carried away and it's somewhat sluggish. Still, I have the advantage of a built-in war club if I run out of darts. (Most original models had no counterweight.)

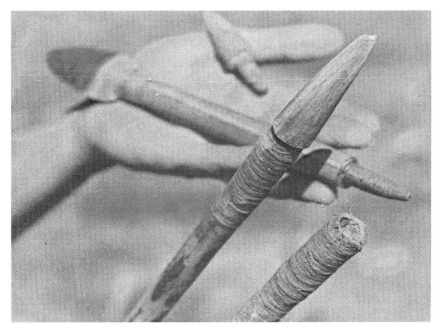

How I cut foreshafts to fit the dart. This way isn't authentic and requires more care in fitting, but it helps more in preventing splitting of the dart when you just might miss your target and hit something more solid. I use antler tips for general shooting. Stone tips would have been used for hunting.

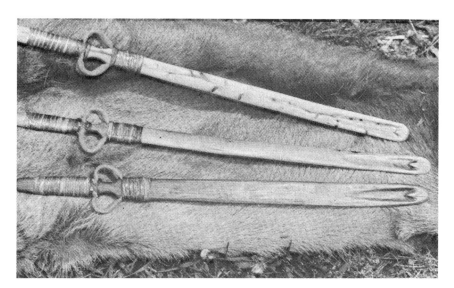

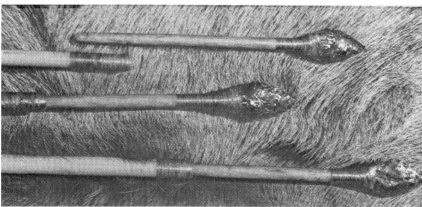

Atlatls and darts done the old way. No counterbalance on the atlatls; foreshafts done the way that they were. These were made by my friend Jim Riggs of Oregon, who also took the photos.

Insects

With insects, more so than with the other critters mentioned up to this point, you may have to really overcome prejudices. To go into any detail as to the edibility of various insects would require a book of its own. (*Butterflies in My Stomach* and *Entertaining with Insects* by Ronald L. Taylor are two good sources; both are out of print but can be found in many libraries.) I include here much useful information on the eating of many common insects. For more details and information on nutritional values I recommend the above books.

Grasshoppers, crickets, and termites, oh my!—all are edible. Earthworms, yeah! Maggots, too. *Most* grubs. Just about any water insects. Caterpillars, *generally* (but avoid the hairy ones, or any brightly colored ones, or those with a disagreeable odor). In fact, the above rules of brightly colored and strong, disagreeable odors should be pretty much followed anywhere in nature. It's nature's way of warning off predators—including us!

Wings and legs should be removed from most, such as the grasshoppers and crickets, since they're hard to digest. I would cook any insect that I had my eye on eating. I've heard from some that this is unnecessary, but I still have that slight fear of parasites. Drying and grinding them into a paste or flour and eating them, or adding them to soups or stews, are other ways to include this nutrition to your diet. (See Chapter 7 for various methods of cooking in a primitive situation.) If you're worried about eating the contents of these critters' intestines, just impound them somewhere for a few hours and they'll empty themselves out. A favorite of many students, especially kids, is grasshoppers, the legs pulled off, cooked on a hot rock, with a texture similar to shrimp.

To help overcome your prejudice of eating insects, just remember that they eat leaves and grasses—and do you know what chickens and hogs eat?

Meat Preservation

Once you've stocked up on provisions, you'll also need to know how to preserve some of your excess for the days that you have nothing—either for the long, late-winter nights or for a journey. The simplest and easiest primitive method is simply to air dry it. Just about anything can be preserved by drying, even watermelon (though you might not have much left when done).

In this chapter, we're thinking mostly about meats. In other words, jerky. What the aboriginal and early settlers used for trail foods and emergency food stores was known as jerked meat. This was simply meat, cut into thin strips (I've read that 1/4" or less thickness will keep the flies from blowing, laying eggs, on it; experience has proved this out), laid over racks and sun dried.

If the weather was wet, meat was dried slowly in the smoke of the fire (which, by the way, was the only time that the early folks flavored their jerky—from the smoke—and that wasn't intentional). After a day or two or three, the meat had been dried (jerked) and was ready for storage, usually in rawhide containers to protect it from moisture. If kept dry, it would literally last forever. All the meat loses through this drying process is moisture. All nutrition remains, but remember, it has no fats.

The jerky can be chewed as is (and chewed, and chewed, and chewed), or it can be, and most often was, pounded and boiled and added to a stew, into which you threw various roots, seeds, bugs, or whatever.

In a more stable situation, other than overnight stops during a journey, the one step further, and a method of preservation a thousand times more valuable, was to make the jerked meat into pemmican. This is done very simply by pounding the dried meat, shredding it apart, and mixing it with fats. This is the ultimate in trail food. On it alone, one can live.

The suet fats of animals are simmered. The pure fat will rise to the top. Here you want to use the hard fat from animals such as deer, buffalo, or beef. The resulting product is tallow (using pork, raccoon, bear, and similar critters produces lard, which is too soft). The prepared jerky is mixed with the tallow and you have the complete meal. This can be, and was, kept in rawhide containers, with all edges sealed with tallow (to ensure that moisture was kept from the meat). It too is forever preserved.

Just be cautious to have the tallow "not hot" when mixing with meat. I like it just shy of setting up—still pourable. If set up too much, it will be difficult to completely cover or coat all the meat. The addition of dried berries and so on will add a better flavor to the greasy meat, as well as carbohydrates.

> *If you use hot tallow, it will cook the meat, which can lead to spoilage and POSSIBLY DEATH!*

Venison strips and packrats drying in the sun.

Left: Beef suet as taken from the critter, then diced to render.

Right: Rendering. The mixture is cooked till completely dissolved, strained, and then the remaining "junk" allowed to settle. The result is clear (white when cooled) tallow.

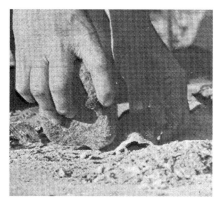

Left: *Pounding dried venison (jerky).*

Right: *The resulting powder. It could be added to stews as is.*

Left: *All the ingredients for "Wasna"—pemmican. Note the tallow, jerky, suet, and a rawhide envelope in which to put the finished product.*

Right: *Pouring tallow into the pounded jerky. Be certain that the tallow has cooled before mixing with the meat, or you will cook it—and rotted cooked meat CAN and WILL poison you!*

Left: *Finished mixing. I don't get too carried away with tallow, just enough to thoroughly coat the meat.*

Right: *Packing into rawhide envelope.*

The filled envelope, packed with nourishment. It's nothing but dried meat mixed with some tallow — all you need to stay alive. The envelope sides (where it's been sewn with sinew) have also been dipped into the tallow to further protect the contents, and a layer of tallow has been poured over the top of the pemmican.

Chapter 6

Deer from Field to Freezer

Say you've shot your deer, or killed it with a bow and arrow or brought it down with some other tool. What next!?

The quality of wild game (or even domesticated) meats begins right here. The first thing that you have to do is to remove the insides. The longer that these remain in the carcass, the more chance there is for spoilage. Once a critter dies, it immediately begins to spoil. We have to stop this action if we want the meat to taste anything like decent.

If an animal's properly shot in the first place (in head, neck, or chest cavity), the removal of the insides is a fairly clean job. With a gut-shot animal, the procedures shown still apply but the job won't be very pleasant.

Removal of the guts not only keeps any extra, adverse tastes from entering the meat but, more important, it *begins cooling the carcass,* which will slow down the decaying process, though only temporarily.

Cooling the carcass is my first action. I do this by immediately field-dressing the game. Then, especially if the weather is warm, by removing the skin from the animal. With deer this is vitally important, as their hollow hair acts as an insulation that keeps heat from leaving the carcass. Virtually the only time that I refrain from immediately removing the skin is when the temperature dips well below freezing and I really don't want the carcass to freeze.

Some people "hang" their animal for periods ranging from a few days for up to two weeks. We do this, too, if the weather permits. I feel that hanging has nothing to do with the taste of the meat. What happens,

I think, is that the meat fibers are allowed to "relax," somewhat acting as a tenderizer, especially good for big old bucks. But for this to be successful, the temperature needs to be approximately 38° to 40°F. If warmer, the meat will begin to rot, and if frozen it'll do no good.

Most all people intentionally in the wilderness will have with them a knife of sorts. Many people have with them *too* much knife. A deer can be field-dressed or skinned and cut up by using nothing more that a fingernail file. I'll illustrate here the entire process, using not a fingernail file but a few stone blades that we knocked from a piece of local chert. I do this to show that if *we* can do the complete process using nothing but a piece of stone, *you* certainly can do it using any or all the modern tools available to you.

The basic principles shown here can also apply to just about any other animal, from squirrel to buffalo.

Field Dressing

Here we have a nice doe—shot not more than a few minutes ago, in the chest. If possible, I like to place the animal on an incline, head down, so that gravity pushes the guts out of the way while I work. Note that the hind legs have already been partially skinned for attachment of the tag, from the fish and game department, through the hind tendons. Laid out are several stone blades. The round rocks are for resharpening if necessary. The bone knives we never did use, but they would also have worked.

Our purpose now is to open the animal from one end to the other, from anus to throat, and remove all that lies in between. You'll soon see that it's all attached and that "pulling the cord" from either end will remove it all. Here, we'll pull from the throat back, though just the reverse will do as well.

Place rocks or sticks on either side of the animal to keep it lying upright on its back.

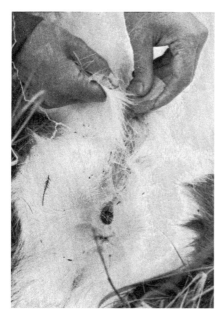

Making the first incision, then carefully pulling the skin out so as not to cut through the stomach lining.

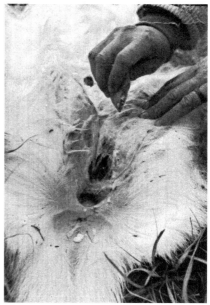

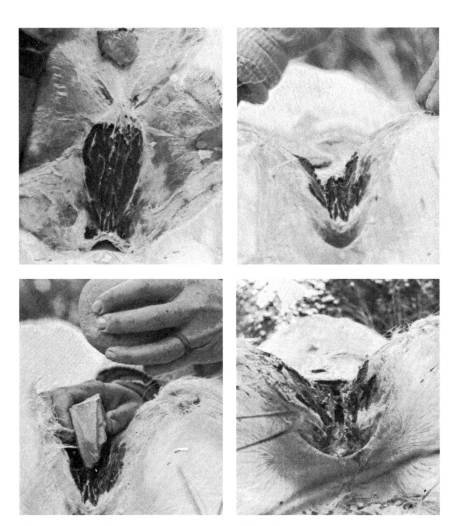

After having cut through the skin for about 6" to 8" up from the anus, we have cut here through the meat down to the pelvic bone. You can readily feel the pointed ridge of the pelvis, which we'll split to free the bowel. Here some people take a long-bladed "sharp" knife and reach through the anal opening and make a circular cut to free this. I've always found splitting the bone much easier. We here illustrate using a sharp-edged rock to do the splitting (a regular hunting knife will make this much easier). When splitting the bone, force the legs apart and with just a slight tap of some sort of hammer, on most deer, it will seem to fall apart. You have to cut in exactly the right spot, on top of the ridge where you can feel where the bone is "welded" together, otherwise you'll be "cutting" and not "splitting." You'll also need to cut just slightly through the stomach membrane right above the pelvis to relieve the tension preventing you from forcing it apart, taking care not to cut through the innards.

Many accounts have you tying off the end of the bowel. We just don't mess with this. If you're careful, nothing will spill out, and if it does it's nothing but firm pellets that won't have a tendency to contaminate. You do as you wish.

Once this delicate task has been taken care of, cut carefully all the way to the throat. If the animal was placed on an incline as noted earlier, the guts won't tend to spill out and thereby get in your way. If an incline just isn't there, place wood, rocks, or whatever under the hind end. You do want to be careful not to cut into the innards. Normally I'll first split the skin, then open the stomach cavity.

You won't be able to open the sternum (breastbone) merely by slicing. With a steel knife you need to stand over the animal, facing its head, and thrust upward. All except the biggest and oldest of animals will split this way. Illustrated here, we split with a sharp-edged stone, then hammer with a wooden club. Then we cut the animal's throat to free the windpipe. (I don't bleed my game. Once a deer is dead, its heart stops beating and the blood stops flowing, unlike a pig, which will spurt blood for many minutes.)

Now, before we begin to take it apart, we need to cut out the diaphragm, which separates the chest and stomach cavities. Just cut it free from the walls—no big deal.

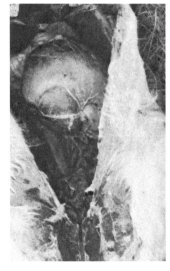

Now we're ready to pull out all the innards. As mentioned before, you can pull from either end. Here we show pulling with the windpipe, using the knife for most of the way to free it from along the backbone. At this stage it's easier to turn the animal sideways on the incline. With little effort the guts will fall out.

If there's snow on the ground, I'll now turn the animal over and let it drain and also cool. Unless the animal has been shot in the guts, the inside of the carcass will be as clean as it should be. If snow isn't available, I'll rinse with cold water, first chance I get, to help cool it if the temperature is up.

The animal is now field-dressed.

Skinning

The next chore is to skin the animal. I was first taught to skin a deer while it lay on the ground, a technique that works well. The main problem with this is that it requires constant bending, which is tough on my bad back (maybe on yours too?). Instead, first split the legs to the center line and then push, pull, fist, or cut the skin off. First do one side to the backbone, and then roll the animal over onto the skin already loosened and repeat on the other side.

I hang most all the deer that I skin from the hind legs, kept spread apart with a stick, after I've first split the skin of the legs up the center to the already split belly.

After these initial opening cuts, the knife can be put aside. By pulling and fisting (pulling the skin with one hand while pushing the fist of the other between skin and carcass), the skin will separate readily from the carcass, especially if the critter's still warm.

Left: Pulling skin from hams.
Right: Pulling over tail.

Left: Cutting skin from tail (I almost never leave the tail on the skin for tanning).
Right: Cutting the tail loose from the body.

Both photos showing fisting the skin off. A bit of extra care is taken around the front shoulder (**right**), as here the layers of meat and membrane tend to overlap.

Pulling skin from front legs,

Deer parted from its coat,

Removing Head

No saw is needed in any of this. Removing the head is simple: Find where the head swivels, where the neck and head meet; then cut through the meat to the bone.

Twist and snap.

Cut loose any remaining membrane and tendons.

Cutting Off Legs

Here I'll show you a simple method of removing the legs, taught to me by an old butcher friend of mine, Argel Pultz of Riley, Kansas. You need actually only follow the series of photos, as they're pretty self-explanatory.

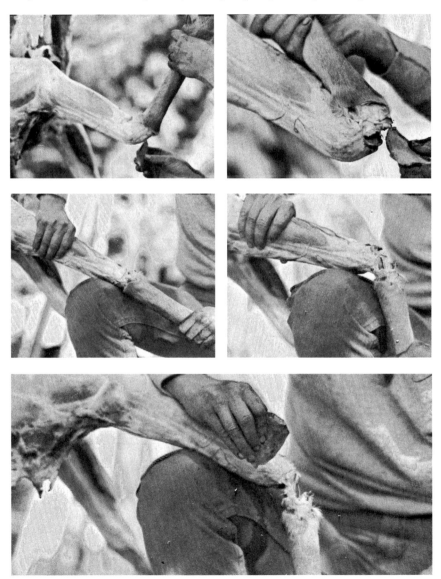

Sinew Removal

If you're following or practicing primitive skills at all, you'll want to save the deer's sinew. It has a great many uses, as explained elsewhere in this book.

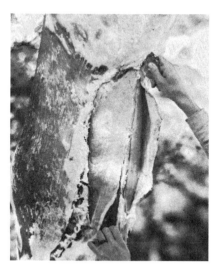

Left: Cutting through outer layer of fat next to backbone, on both sides.

Right: Pulling away layer of fat exposing sinew as shiny silver membrane (tendon) covering loins.

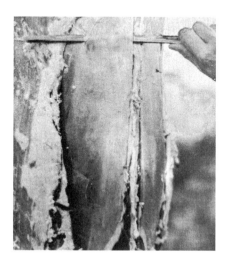

Left: Putting stick (we generally use a dull knife) between sinew and loin meat.

Right: Pulling down with a smooth motion while jiggling the stick to separate sinew cleanly from the loin.

Left: Using stick to clean strip as much as possible before removal.

Right: Pushing fingers down following sinew strip to separate it from meats, on both sides.

Left: A slight tug will pull free the strip at the shoulder (cutting it here loses 2" to 3").

Right: Cutting free at the hip where the sinew draws into a cord.

Removing Loin and Tenderloin

The bestest of the best. Loins or tenderloins, or both, cut into butterfly steaks.

*After removing the sinew, the loins are what lie underneath. Removing (**left**) is simple. A knife's hardly needed. The loins can simply be pulled loose (though a knife makes a neater job of it). The tenderloin is the smaller strip of meat lying against the backbone on the inside (**right**); this also can be pulled loose, though again a knife makes it neater.*

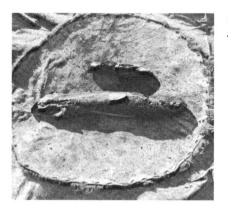

One each of the strips, showing relative size.

Cutting into thick steaks.

Cutting these again to make them "butterflies."

Butterflies cut from one each loin and tenderloin.

Cutting Up of Carcass

You'll next want to cut up the deer carcass.

Removing a shoulder. The knife will find its own way.

Separating side meat from hindquarters.

Cutting away hindquarter. Again, the blade will find its own way. But here you'll have a socket to cut out and separate.

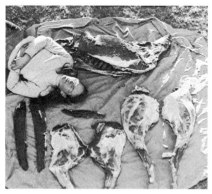

Pieces—and cutter—all laid out.

Meat Cutting

We bone all our meat, and that's what we'll show on these pages.

Geri with hindquarter.

Hindquarter laid out, with the first two cuts made.

All meat separated from bones.

Hindquarter: bone, steaks, and roasts.

Geri with front shoulder.

Boned.

*Front shoulder:
bone, roasts,
and stew meat.*

Geri with main body.

*Excess meats removed,
for ham (deer) burger, or
(for us) stew.*

Cutting meat from ribs. We prepare boneless ribs and enjoy them thoroughly. Meat from here could also be used as stew or deerburger.

The clean carcass, with a pile of rib meat and meat for stew or burger.

And that, folks, is all there is to it. It's really very simple. We don't begin to pretend that we're butchers—far from it. But, as Geri says, all that really matters is to get the meat small enough to fit into the frying pan.

Go to it!

Chapter 7

Primitive Wilderness Cooking Methods

What's behind the resurgence of interest in primitive living? For Geri and me, it's a freedom gained from reliance on others—freedom from dependency. Every person living in this world, or even out of it (in the space shuttle even now circling the globe and looking down on our present somewhat-dire condition), is dependent on the Earth for his or her existence. It don't matter who or where you are, the Earth supplies your wants and needs (or doesn't, if you're among the unfortunate many).

Geri's thought—that everyone should be compelled to visit a slaughterhouse at least once during their growing years—is a good one. It's mind-boggling how many people think that everything just automatically comes prepackaged.

Like it or not, we are a part *of* the Earth, not something separate from it. Face it: *We are animals*. The only thing that differentiates us from other animals is our ability to reason, for we are (supposedly) intelligent. If all man-made things quit at one time, the Earth wouldn't be bothered with the overpopulation of humans anymore. It seems that many are searching, realizing the sad situation that we've gotten ourselves into and trying to do at least a little bit about it. Just *knowing* the everyday skills explained in this book can free you from your dependency.

This chapter explores various methods of cooking up some of the things that you've been shown how to catch, with no modern-day pots and pans. We'll hit several different methods of cooking something up, but remember: These are only *some* of the methods that will work. There are certainly many that you can come up with yourself, with a little experience and a lot of imagination plus a will to live.

COOK: "to prepare food for eating by heating."
Simple—yeah, really!

For most people today, you take away their pots, pans, electric skillets, and microwaves, and there would be a problem. But, as with any of the other primitive living skills, once you think about it (or have it shown to you), cooking really *is* easy, even out in the wilds.

In the Coals

Most boys of the outdoors, at least in my day, didn't concern themselves with a lot of extra "junk" to carry around. Traveling light was the thing. All we needed was wieners, potatoes, and corn on the cob thrown directly into the coals, plus some sticks to move them around and get them out when ready (and also to scrape off some of the excess ashes). We also sometimes carried a can of beans or stew, and almost always a small pan to heat water, or to melt snow, for coffee or hot chocolate (remember, Dave?)

So. To throw your meal directly into the coals *is* the easiest way to cook up something. A little bit of ashes won't hurt a body, but remember that ashes make lye, and lye will eat *you*. So, for safety sake, a little ashes should go a long way.

Jim Riggs of Oregon, with his students, simply singes the hair off deer mice over flames and throws them directly into the coals till done "just right"—they come out crispy, not too mushy on the inside. Nothing wasted here. They eat the whole thing: a good way to pick up extra vitamins. We mostly just skin, remove the stomach and intestines, then cook and eat what's left. But *beware of hantavirus!*

> **Please see the cautions on hantavirus pulmonary syndrome beginning on page 146.**

Left: The daily special—at least, that day's: a field mouse. Below: After singeing hair off and roasting in coals.

Geri's first bite.

"Can I swallow now?"—it's really awfully dry (overdone?).

If it didn't kill her (and Jim and Marie and whomever), I guess it won't kill me. Remember, this is all mouse—no gutting or skinning.

Packing small game and birds in a mud or clay pack works well, also. Not any old "mud" will work—it needs to be somewhat sticky so that it doesn't crumble apart on you. Get the pack as airtight as possible so as to keep all the juices in. This method has a couple advantages. You don't need to skin, singe, or pluck the game—it all will stick to the mud and fall away from the meat when done. You can also pack tubers and veggies all in the same package. Gutting it is your choice. In a true primitive or survival situation, you may elect to eat it all to get the maximum nourishment that's available (not knowing where your next meal's coming from).

Have you ever cooked corn on the cob directly on the coals at a barbecue? Just dip the ear in water and it will steam as it cooks. The same can be done with other edibles, though be a bit choosy when you pick the greenery to wrap the food in, as flavors will be added to the food. Certain leaves (oak and walnut) can impart a bitter taste. Certainly avoid poison ivy, oak, sumac, and their ilk. And a little sage goes a long way. Sometimes grasses plaited together, or cattail leaves, either green or wetted, will help protect the outside from burning and also kinda steam the meal.

If you have any type of flour, make a dough by mixing it with water. Pat the dough thicker if you want it doughy, thinner for crispy. Throw into the ashes and, presto: You have "ash cakes."

Trout being wrapped in clay or mud.

Sealed mudded trout.

Laid on coals. More raked onto this. (Note oven at far right.)

Finished. The mud or clay pulls away the skin (feathers and skins of birds) and you're left with tasty trout...done just right. You'll hafta guess the time, depending on the coals. This was about 20 minutes.

Broiling

Imagine this romantic scene: a deer, rabbit, or bird skewered onto a stick that's placed onto two forked sticks and supported over the fire.

But, when you turn the stick, the critter stays in the same position, not turning with the stick.

How often I've seen that. It's a great way to cook, yet too often I've met folks who don't know how to keep the meat turning on the stick.

One simple way: Poke a hole (or two) through the *green* stick that skewers the animal. Then run another stick through the animal, the stick, and back out through the animal again. If you don't have a knife, a sharp pointed rock or dead sharp piece of wood (preferably hardwood) should split the green skewer easily enough. With this method you can cook anything from a mouse to a buffalo.

Cornish hen and trout laid out to be spitted. Note holes in skewers and aligned pins.

Hen and trout cooking. Since fire was built on solid rock, we couldn't use sticks as uprights to hold skewers, so we used rocks. We also placed rocks on skewers to keep the meals from rotating and falling to lowest balance.

Overall view of "working" fire.

*Getting kinda crowded. Ash cake in coals (**upper**), dough on stick (**upper right**), venison steak on sticks (**center**), and potatoes and grasshoppers frying on flat rock top of oven (**lower**).*

*A lot of food from one fire. You normally wouldn't use all methods at once, but for photos? At **top** is baked (mud) fish. Right of that is broiled steak. **Center** is hen and trout, rotisseried. **Left** of that are trout and potato baked in oven. At **lower left** are ash cake and bread baked on a stick. To **right** of that are fried potatoes and grasshoppers. To the **extreme right**, the gourmets' delight—roasted mouse.*

Again, if flour is available, wrap your dough directly onto a stick and prop it over the coals.

A steak, roast, fish, or bird can also be stuck onto a green stick and pinned as above. Or you can use two sticks at angles and prop your dinner over the fire or coals. Turn as necessary.

Another trick (from Harry in Troy, Montana): Fold two thin, pliable saplings back on themselves and place your fish, or whatever, inside; then hold or prop it over the fire or coals.

The cooking methods that we've covered up till now are those that you'd figure out pretty quick if the necessity arose. Some, not all, of what we hit now will be things that aren't so often or easily figured out by many.

Baking

Here we're talking not about cakes and pies, but just the same old stuff that we've been cooking up till now. By making an oven (of sorts), we're freed of watching quite so carefully what's going on, so as not to burn supper.

About anytime that we build a cooking fire, at one end we build a small oven of rocks, as flat as we can get them. On those occasions when flat rocks aren't available, a careful choosing, banging, and placing of round rocks will make a serviceable oven.

The fire is built. As it burns down, coals are raked into and around and over the oven. Heat the rocks slowly so that any water that may be inside the stone has a chance to leave…slowly. Heat too fast and the steam may leave too fast, as in *bang!*

We usually build a longish fire (call it a pit fire), with active burning at one end, coals in the middle, and oven at the other end. Our ovens are normally only 3" to 4" high and deep by about 6" wide, larger only if necessary. Smaller ovens are more efficient for small things, such as pieces of meat, potatoes, tubers, veggies, birds, and dough for what amounts to bread. We keep coals in front and on top (and sides too, if it works out, though that's not necessary). In such an oven foods are done as quick as in the oven at home.

Another easy oven is a dirt-bank type. Dig into the base of a dirt bank. If it happens to be clay, fine. If not, line with flat rocks. Build your fire inside and let heat. When it's ready, just scrape out and keep coals or fire at or near the entrance.

Now, in conjunction with the first of these ovens, you have right at hand a frying pan: your hot, flat rock that makes the top of the oven. You can fry about anything here that you can at home (though maybe not over-easy eggs, without lots of practice and luck!).

One other "oven type" way to cook is also a hole in the ground. Dig a hole plenty large enough for what you intend to place in it. You'll want some extra space (note the following photos). There are a lot of variations to this "pit" cooking. You just pick and choose what works for you.

If the soil is claylike, fire it by building a hot fire within. If the soil is sandy or crumbly, line it with flat stones.

Build a fire in the prepared hole. I prefer to leave the coals in the hole. I put a handful of green sticks or twigs directly onto the coals, followed by a layer of green or wetted grass, maybe adding some cattail leaves (green) if available, and then the meal. The green sticks or twigs will add a great smoke flavoring. The wet or green grasses and cattail leaves add moisture and also protect the meal from direct contact with the coals. Do remember, though, that the particular tastes of the leaves and grasses will stay with the meal.

Then in goes the meal: meat, roots, nuts, whatever. Cover the hole with a flat rock that's been preheated and seal. Place coals on the rock. Now the food is heated from above *and* below, with more of a steam heat. Trial and error will dictate the time. Because of the moist heat, you really can't overcook. Figure three to five hours for most average-sized meals.

The fact that oxygen can't fuel the fire will keep the thing from bursting into flames—hence, the importance of covering coals and sealing the hole as fast as possible.

If a flat rock isn't available, build a supporting layer of sticks at the top of the pit and cover it with a jacket, shirt, blanket, or grasses (grasses aren't the best, as they'll leak some dirt). Then proceed to seal this with plenty of dirt. This will also work better if the dirt has been preheated by building a fire over it. Because the pit is sealed *air-tight*, and by taking particular care to cover the coals with moist greenery, no flames *should* appear (though they might).

Now you have several hours to forage or trap or build without having to tend your meal.

Left: *Rock lid being heated.* **Right:** *All laid out: chicken and potatoes (**lower**), green sticks (**middle**), and wet grasses and green wetted cattail leaves (**top**).*

*Left: Green sticks placed directly onto coals (to keep grasses from coming in direct contact). Also note rocks lining the hole, helping to retain heat. **Right:** Placing grasses and cattail leaves in hole.*

*Left: Now in goes the meal and (**right**) laying the rock lid and sealing all openings first with grasses and then with dirt. You want it sealed till no smoke is seen escaping. If air enters, the meal can be burned. We also piled about 6" of dirt on top to help keep in the heat. Since the rock was already hot clear through, we didn't build a fire on top, though it can be done.*

The finished meal. Here we let it cook for only 2 1/2 hours because of failing daylight. Chicken was perfect, just beginning to fall from the bones. The potatoes were done, but firm.

Boiling

One of the best reasons there is for knowing how to boil something in a primitive situation (and there are several such reasons) is to make a little bit go a long way. One smallish piece of meat—say, a rat, a squirrel, a coupla mice, a bird, even fish—when boiled or roasted will help to fill your belly faster than eating the critter raw. And to the broth can be added any number of other nutritious things that you've gathered during the day, such as seeds, nuts, insects, or edible plants. And though it's not the thing that you'd normally be able to accomplish on your first night in a primitive situation, unless you're awfully lucky to find just the right "pot," it also isn't difficult to come across things that can function as a pot.

What we'll do in this situation is to heat the water using hot rocks—called, appropriately, *hot rock cooking*.

Although most rocks will do the job, you do need to be somewhat selective. Some will just crumble (sandstones), but others can and do explode when heated (flints, cherts, obsidian). *You* will need to do the checking if you can't tell the difference. And *do* be aware of the danger of exploding rocks. But just a bit of knowledge and common sense will prevent any mishaps, or at least most.

We assume no responsibility for any injury resulting from exploding rocks.

We generally prefer "creek rocks," but *those not actually found in creeks*. The hard, roundish granite-type stones seem to us to work about the best. Just pick them from higher ground. Those that have been soaked in water might have gotten moisture inside through tiny cracks; when the rock is heated, the water can't get out slowly enough for the crack to accommodate—and so, *bang*.

We've used soft limestone. It heats well but eventually breaks apart (as do all rocks that I've used). Softer rocks also have the tendency to leave a grit in the soup or stew, though that may help to keep your insides reamed out. Pumice or lava rock is a good choice.

Heat the rocks. It's best to build a good, solid foundation of wood on which to build your fire. Reason: All rocks eventually fall into the deepest part of the fire, which may not be the hottest if it happens to be only the ground. Layer wood and rocks. We generally use about a dozen rocks to heat a gallon of water (more or less), as the temperature of the water from a mountain stream is usually awfully cold. As the first rocks are taken from under the water as they cool, place them in a section of "new" fire. When you run out of rocks the first time through and you're not done cooking, the first ones used will have heated again and be ready to go. The second section of fire also helps to distinguish which rocks are which.

The pot: We've often used a fresh deerskin for our pot. Either set it into a hole in the ground and stake it around, or tie it into a tripod of sticks. Usually the hair's left on. We generally cook this way when demonstrating brain tanning, and we use the freshly fleshed (say *that* 10 times fast!) skin, hair side out of course. You don't need to flesh the skin, as the flesh and fats will add to the meal. The skin will shrink considerably as *it* also cooks, so take this into account or you'll have broth all over the place. We normally leave lots of slack in the skin when cooking in a hole. Tied to a tripod, it'll just shrink, so don't fill it as full. You'll hafta feel this out.

A larger animal's stomach can be, and has been, used also. Here you have the added advantage of being able to eat the pot.

A depression large enough in a rock would be great, as long as it's convenient for and to camp.

A solid piece of wood will work fine, though it will take some time to hollow it out (it's easiest done with fire). In a semipermanent camp, this would be no problem.

A clay pot is the cat's meow. This could also be just placed into the fire. (See Chapter 9 for more details on primitive pottery.)

A tightly coiled basket will work as a pot. I've always thought that such baskets needed to be lined with pitch, but have been shown otherwise by those who know.

A hole dug in the ground (ground that wouldn't leak) would surely work. So much the better if the ground happened to be clayish. Build a fire in it first, and you've got a nonmovable pot.

Now, let's get cooking.

When we first started hot rock cooking, we just used forked sticks and placed the hot rocks directly into the skin pot. By carefully removing the rocks from the pot, we were able to get two or three meals out of one skin. Finally, a hole would appear in the weakened skin, and our supper (the broth, anyhow) literally went down the drain.

We now make a small basket or carrier to put the rocks into and then place that in the pot. This is *much* easier on the pot. You can sometimes place three or four rocks into the carrier. It's best to have the carrier in the soup before putting the hot rocks in, as they have a tendency to burn through the cordage holding it together, since the rocks are red hot, or near to it.

The following photos show the tools we normally use, but remember, forked sticks alone will do.

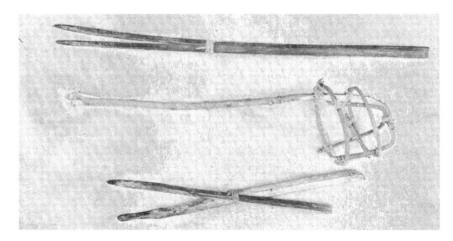

*Tools handy for hot rock cooking. Two types of "tongs" (**top and bottom**) and a basket to hold the rocks while immersing into the skin pot. This saves wear and tear on the pot when taking rocks out. Simple forked sticks can be used in lieu of tongs.*

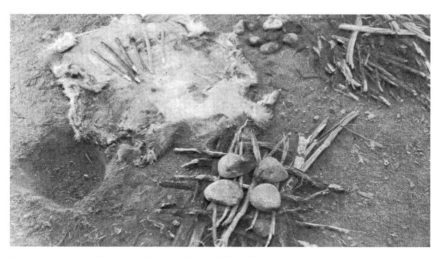

Everything is gathered and ready for boiling. Hole dug; deerskin and stakes; rocks and wood; and rocks and wood layered ready to be fired.

I know that cooked meat can poison you if it spoils, and the rawhide pot *does* cook. I don't know how to judge this, but common sense should dictate here, so don't let the "cooked" pot get too old.

It normally takes from 5 to 10 fist-sized rocks, red hot, to bring the water to a boil. Remember, this is usually mountain creek water, which is mighty cold! Figure about 10 minutes or less. Once boiling, it only takes one or two rocks in the basket at a time to keep the brew simmering for 3 to 5 minutes. When these are first placed in the brew it'll boil like a hot springs, and then settle down to a simmer. You can hear the rocks cooking and sizzling. When it slows down, take the rocks out and replace with new ones. You'll be cooking as fast as you would on a stove. In fact, the water will boil hotter at higher elevations and so cook faster. I know of one fellow who does all his camp boiling with hot rocks (in a Dutch oven) while in the mountains just because it does cook faster. And if you saw the size of this guy, you'd know why he wanted or needed his food faster!

Skin staked out and filled with water. Skin will shrink considerably while boiling, so extra slack is left in hole. Rocks heating in background.

When rocks have heated, the fire is stretched out so that when cool rocks are removed from the vat they can be reheated, while also keeping the two batches of rocks separate.

Using "tongs" to place hot rocks into basket, in the water to help keep burning through the basket.

Rocks in basket in broth.

After several rocks (in this case, about 10) are placed in the water, it comes quickly to a rolling boil and will simmer for 3 to 5 minutes.

I'll touch on one other method to (kinda) boil things. For quite some time we've used dehaired deer rawhide for water buckets. I've seen water boiled in a paper cup that's placed directly into a fire. Take note that paper and deer rawhide aren't the same.

The pot or bucket at first will leak readily. After some soaking (from a few to several hours), it somehow seals itself. One bucket that we've carried for over a year and always fill with water at workshops and demos doesn't "leak" at all, though water does filter through and evaporate (thereby keeping the contents cool).

Well, one summer we carried around a pot of deer rawhide—a nice skin, too—with the intention of cooking in it. We did. First we got lots of coals but little flame. Our pot is held together by natural fiber cordage, and several times flames were licking close. It was a hassle. And the skin kept springing leaks (dripping): no rhyme or reason, just when and wherever they felt like it. And then they'd quit. Not enough to put the fire out (just drips), but a real pain. It kept the fire cool. We worked for about two hours and never did get the damn thing to *boil*. It did simmer, and would have cooked after the first 15 or 20 minutes or so. But boil—no. It also shrank to almost half its original size. We had to constantly dip water out. Hot rocks work much better.

Rawhide bucket directly over the coals. It works... but. If no rocks were available, this would be a good second choice, though ruining a good skin.

Water dripping from rawhide pot.

Chapter 8

Primitive Wilderness Containers

No hunters or gatherers are worth their salt without something to put their gatherings in. As with most other aspects of primitive living, assembling a suitable container is actually much easier than you might at first suspect, what with all the cumulative knowledge that you've gained in reading about other aspects of primitive living in the other chapters. The importance of some suitable container can't be stressed enough—it really *does* make life easier. Remember, you're going "naked into the wilderness," and you've got no pockets.

I designed this chapter to show you a lot of photos with some descriptive and explanatory words. I figure that the photos pretty well speak for themselves. This material, however, is far from the final word on containers. Instead, what you'll encounter here are several types that have worked for Geri and me and that are primarily *functional,* with little or no artwork. There are many, many ideas that will work as well but that we haven't covered, due not only to lack of space but also to our own lack of knowledge. We do show workable products, and—most importantly—we explain the characteristics that you need to look for to get the job done in your own region of the country.

Baskets

The first container that comes to mind to most folks would be a basket. Here we'll show you three methods to obtain some sort of basket. While the instructions in this chapter will be far from definitive answers to your every question on basketry, they do offer three ways that work well to give you a finished product. You don't need to stick to any one of these methods but can mix and match, as you will and as the circumstances dictate. To all you artists in basketry out there, please bear with us and remember that these are *functional*.

Materials

As will be shown, many things in nature work well in basketry. You only need to search out particular characteristics—mainly that a material is pliable, or can be made to be. It helps if it'll remain a bit pliable after the project has been completed so that it won't fall apart in use. The purpose of the basket will help to dictate this. If it's to be used only for gathering nuts (the ones growing on trees, not those living in them) or herbs, a lighter-duty basket will suffice. If your goal is to gather heavy-duty rocks or whatever (and remember, we cavemen do need our rocks!), then a brittle basket will be wasted. The longer the material is, the less splicing will be necessary to create a basket.

Stick baskets—as I refer to those made of, well, sticks—can and should be made more pliable by soaking for several hours or days, depending on the material. We mostly use *dogwood* and *willow* for these. You can use the information in this chapter as a guide, but *do* search out your area to find what it has to offer, and then maybe experiment or temporize. As you'll see, many other materials can be and are used—cattails; any cordage; some vines, barks, and grasses. As we approach these various materials herein, we'll explain how to prepare them.

Warps, Wefts, and Woofs

These are what your baskets are composed of. *Warps* are the longitudinal threads, sticks, or cords into which the *wefts* (also known as *woofs*) are threaded. This is a simple definition, and in practice the actual basket is sometimes not so simply accomplished.

Top right: Note that an additional warp has been added (**lower center, arrow**). As we proceed, you'll find that warps will be added as necessary for strength.

Middle left: Note the splicing in of a new weft (the upper arrow shows the last of the old; the lower arrow points to the new).

Middle right: Note, on the far side, how the warps have been threaded down into the wefts to finish. Another cord has been wrapped around the perimeter for added strength

Bottom: The finished product.

Twining

In twining, you're working with two wefts. Normally you twist these once, between warps.

 With this basket (actually, here a bag), shown in the process of being made, we're using cattails exclusively as the material. These were cut dead in winter, and allowed to dry (cattails grow where it's wet), and resoaked, then corded for the warps. The cording allows for a stronger basket or bag. (Cording is taught in detail in Chapter 1.) Then a single piece of cattail, wet, was twined in.

This bag, also twined, has been made from a variety of materials. Elm bark was corded for the warps, while the bottom coupla inches was single-strand elm bark, followed by a few inches of western dogbane, followed by several more inches of eastern dogbane (not corded; the fibers only cleaned and then twined in). The whole was finished at the top with several inches of grass—what we call slough grass, since it grows in wet areas, and what others call reed canary grass.

The strap is brain-tanned deerskin (finished according to methods given in Chapter 10).

This burden basket, appropriately named, is made mostly from dogwood, with a bit of willow tossed in. Deer rawhide supports the basket, to which is tied a tumpline (pack strap) of brain-tanned deerskin. The tumpline goes around the shoulders or the head when carrying, leaving the hands free.

Basket Weave

To basket weave means, of course, to weave a basket.

There are many ways in which you can begin your warps (your up and downers). This step is almost always the most difficult. You'll never have nearly enough hands for this operation. Sticks are always wanting to fall apart here. Just persevere and it'll work.

Now, when basket weaving, you need to have an *odd* number of warps, for the weaving to work out. With twining it makes no difference.

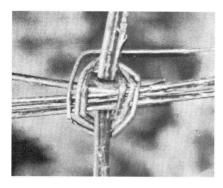

Note the addition of a 13th warp in the upper left.

Geri did most all the basket work illustrated on these pages. She simply laid 3 shoots (of willow) on 3 others (making for 12 warps). She then made several wraps using the basket weave, which is simply one over and the next under the warp. Then she stuck another shoot in, in order to make an odd number, and from here on out the basket weave achieves its purpose, alternating one above and one below on each full turn. After only a few wraps she decided to bend the shoots upward, to make for a more cylindrical basket.

How warps are added in as we go.

Showing how to bend the ends of the shoots over and shove them into the space provided next to the next warp—got that? Naturally, cut the shoots just a coupla inches long for this.

*The finished basket, with (**right**) the addition of a cordage strap.*

*Here we have quite a combination. Using willow (**left**), we begin with the one-strand basket weave, changing to a two-strand twining (**right**).*

Left: *The same, seen from the side.*

Right: *The completed basket, using slough grass, wetted, in a basket weave the rest of the way. Result: a surprising useful basket, much stronger than you'd expect.*

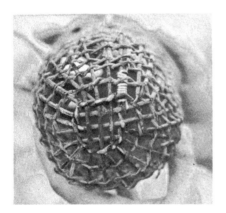

Side and bottom views: *A variation of twining that's very useful in baskets that can use spacing, such as fish traps. (This was made for and sent to us by a master basket-maker friend of ours in California who wishes to remain anonymous.)*

Coiled Basket

You'll have to closely study all the following photos, remembering that starting is the hardest part of all. Here we're using only slough grass and tying it together with yucca fibers, though almost any cordage-type material would suffice.

The middle photo on the right shows Geri opening a passageway for the yucca, using a bone awl.

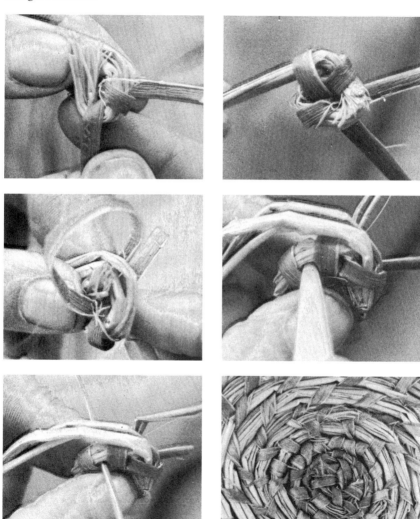

Top: *Ending off a piece of yucca and bringing it under the preceding two loops.*

Middle: *From the inside of basket at same tie-off, beginning with a new strand.*

Bottom: *Showing, from the outside, beginning anew after the initial tie-in.*

How to tie off, or finish, the basket.

Bottom right: Flint blade to be used in cutting off loose ends.

The finished basket.

Bark Container

In the field, you can use bark in a surprising number of ways. The one that interests us here is the making of containers. Using bark is one of the quickest means of making a finished container. What we illustrate in the photos is working with *eastern red cedar*. The first priority in selecting bark is that it easily separates from the tree. The second is that it isn't so fragile and brittle that it'll self-destruct. Most of us know that *birch* bark works for any number of containers, including the famous canoe of poems and stories. The first "other" bark container that I was presented with was made of *juniper* (one of which is illustrated later). Another useful bark is that of the *tulip poplar*. Many species of *elm* work well. Experiment.

Since the photos are self-explanatory, I'll list here the more important aspects to be aware of. You'll note that any holes are *drilled* into the bark, not cut. The bark really wants to split, so care must be taken. When the container's finished, place it over an object that will force it to keep its shape as it dries. Here we used a log.

Also note that in the two photos where Geri ties the container together, each is done differently. One uses a series of holes with cordage run through in such a way that there's a hole for the cord to run through, and also the cord runs around the container. In the other photo, there's only a single tie at the top and the rest is held together with cord. The pointed sides of the bottoms make it easy to tie the cordage off there, adding more strength.

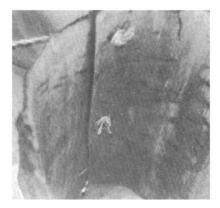

Left: Two bark containers made by and given to us by our friends Ken and Lynn Berry of Alabama, using tulip poplar. Note the wooden handle on the one on the left and also how they're tied.

Right: Container made from juniper, tied with brain tan, to make a fine quiver (made by our friend Brian James of Washington State).

Cordage

We covered cordage in depth in Chapter 1, so we won't go into it again here, except to note that, though not necessarily a "container," cordage can sure haul a lot of stuff on a gathering expedition. In many circumstances, it can also be made on the spot.

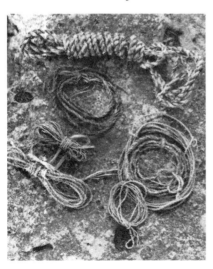

Note a variety of cordage made from natural materials (**left**) and also the general carryall using it (**right**).

Stone Container

Some stones are soft enough to work with. The accompanying photos show soapstone being used to create containers. This material works super easily and was used extensively in days of old, where it was available.

> **Beware: Soapstone sometimes contains asbestos, which can be harmful to your health.**

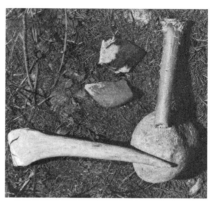

Top left: *Soapstone beginning to be worked.*

Top right: *Working materials of bone, antler, sharp cutting stones, and a hammerstone.*

Bottom left: *Geri hard at it.*

Bottom right: *The finished container.*

We've also used limestone for containers (our Kentucky limestone, not what's found in the Southeast). Though it can be used for hot rock cooking, it won't withstand the higher temperature of being placed directly into the fire.

Top left: *A beautiful soapstone bowl on the left, a gift from Steve Watts of Gastonia, North Carolina (ours is on the right).*

Top right: *Our finished product, an oil lamp, filled with deer tallow (cooked with prickly pear cactus to keep it firmer) and using a sage bark wick.*

Bottom: *What can happen if you're not careful.*

Animal Parts Used as Containers

The animal kingdom sure does provide us with an abundance of spare parts, many of which we can use as containers. Our ancestors did it, and so can you. Here we'll delve into several of them, beginning with the outside.

Rawhide—Such a variety of containers can be made from the raw hide of the animal that it staggers the imagination.

Left: *Buffalo rawhide laid out with a pair of parfletche, traditionally two to a hide.*

Right: *A container made from the raw skin of a deer, leaving the hair on, for holding our firemaking kit.*

Parfletche—This was the Plains Indians' suitcase. All types of containers can be made from a heavy hide: round, square, rectangular, what-have-you. They can be held together in any number of ways, such as by sewing, tying, or gluing, or in combination. But rawhide becomes an oozing mass when wetted, so you must take care to waterproof anything made from it, or otherwise protect it from moisture. We size (varnish) our products with the juice of the prickly pear. Several other waterproofing options are available that we won't cover in this book.

A container that can be used for several purposes. It's simply rawhide of a deer, laced to a wooden frame. Most obviously, this could be used for water or hot rock cooking (see Chapter 7).

Left: *An unborn calf rawhide with gussets of rawhide deer, laced together with brain tan.*

Right: *Deer rawhide with gussets and lacing of brain tan.*

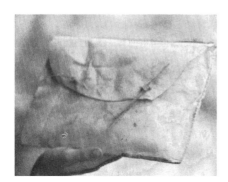

Left: *Deer rawhide container that we use to carry many things, from arrowheads to granola, sewn with sinew (Chapter 10) and tied with brain tan.*

Right: *Knife sheath made from buffalo rawhide, laced with brain tan.*

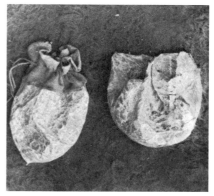

Left: *A cow's bladder, after cleaning the "p" out of it, makes a dandy canteen; carrier made of brain tan. The water bucket next to it we've used for several years, made of a deerskin that we make certain to dry every night so it doesn't begin to rot. The evaporation of the water through the skin keeps it surprisingly cool.*

Right: *Two heart sacs from cows. To prepare, same as with bladders, let them dry, moistening and manipulating them carefully as they dry. They make good, waterproof containers. Sac at left has brain tan sewn on top.*

Left: *Raw squirrel skin, made somewhat flexible by rubbing while it dried—with wooden cork.*

Right: *Skin inverted, cork inserted in neck, cordage to tie the bottom together, and we have a dandy small bag for trap triggers and other uses.*

A much larger bag can be made from this coyote or almost any other big animal.

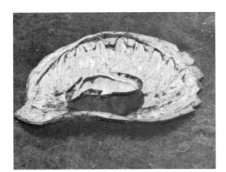

Left: *Two turtle shells, which have many uses: as dishes, water carriers, dippers, cups, or (in the case of the smaller, deeper one) a fine oil lamp.*

Right: *The leg bone of a bear, filled with a tallow-soaked wick and tallow, makes a great torch.*

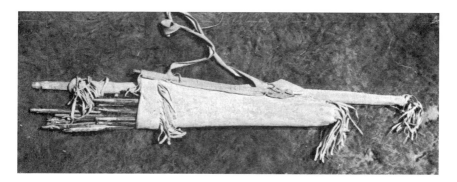

Finished-out buckskin makes for many swell containers. Illustrated is a typical Northern Plains bow case and quiver.

Wood Container

Most containers made of wood are associated with bowls for eating, or as dippers or buckets. In most cases, a container of one piece of wood is too heavy or is prone to break, or both. Canoes, consisting of dug-out logs, would be an exception.

A solid, dry piece of a softwood can be chipped, carved, or burned out to make most of the above items. One caution, though, when burning: If moisture remains in the wood, the high temperature of the burning coal can cause the expanding steam to crack the wood.

Drinking bowl made by burning, chipping, and scraping.

Now, here's something a bit different. Many woods, especially soft cottonwood logs, when left out to weather, *rot from the inside out.*

I discovered this fact while gathering punky wood for smoking skins. The insides were well rotted while the outside (having been sunbaked) was still reasonably hard.

Find the "just right" piece of wood and you can carefully break away an area that you can use—a container ready to be made.

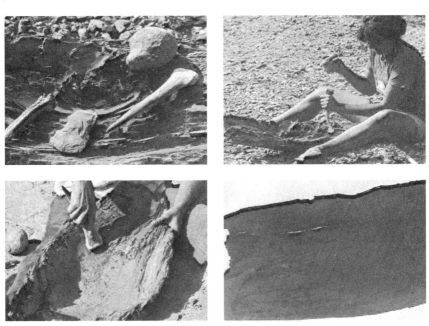

Top left: *About the same tools used in working the stone (preceding section).*

Top right: *Geri hard at it. Actually, the rotted wood separates easily.*

Bottom left: *She smoothes out her work.*

Bottom right: *A major crack shows in the wood (there were also several smaller bug holes).*

Top left: *Fine cordage-type material and a small hunk of clay.*

Top right: *These items mixed together.*

Left: *Geri patches the crack as if caulking a log cabin, sealing the smaller round bug holes as well (though some holes were sealed by jamming in sticks of the appropriate size).*

The finished container, holding 1 1/2 to 2 quarts of water. The seals held up real well for several hours and even through a hot rock cooking session.

Now you've seen *many* and *varied* means to obtain or make containers in the wilds. More important, you possess the *knowledge of just what to look for* when you want to go a-gatherin'. Knowing and understanding the principles and characteristics of what you're doing and looking for is vastly more important than knowing only how one or two methods or materials work—and much better than having any kit.

Chapter 9

Primitive Pottery

This chapter certainly is not a definitive work on primitive pottery. What it *will* do is give you some ideas and techniques for going out, digging up some dirt (clay), and turning it into a usable container or vessel to make your wilderness living or survival more bearable.

As always when trying new things, expect some failures. (Along our journeys, we had a great many, but lived to tell about it!) This material contains a lot of variables, though if you understand the principles and follow the rules, success will follow—for many people, this will happen on the very first try.

Quick Run-Through

Simply, you need to:

- Find a source of clay.
- Dig it up.
- Wet it, if dry.
- Clean it.
- Form it into a shape (a bowl, in our example here).
- Let it dry.

At this stage, it can be used under limited and controlled circumstances. It will be very brittle and will dissolve if wetted. Clay, when mixed with straw and baked in the sun, can be and has been used over millennia to make bricks (adobe). Bowls can be used for *dry* storage. But for most practical applications the item must now be fired. Only fire will transform the water-soluble clay into a material that will enable you to use the bowl, not only to store water but also to boil it.

It really is about that simple. Let's cover the above steps, maybe amplifying and adding one or two others as we go.

Clay

Without getting technical, clay is a type of soil that (1) when moist becomes plastic (that is, moldable); (2) dries hard, retaining its molded shape; and (3) will change characteristics when fired, so that it won't dissolve once again when wetted. Firing allows a clay bowl, for example, to be used as a cooking and storage vessel, and lets you create lots of other utilitarian as well as fun things, both cheaply and quickly.

Most everyone knows what clay is. You just have to find some. It really is a rather abundant earth material. You'll most often and easily find clay deposits along stream banks, next to ponds, and in road cuts.

Clay, like Geri in this photo, can sometimes be elusive—but it's really quite abundant.

Before wetting dry clay, it's best to first pound or grind it into smaller pieces.

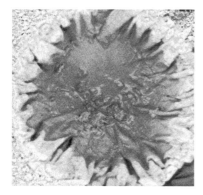

Leftover rubble.

*The more approved method of cleaning: making into a slurry (**left**),
then pouring off the thinner clay (**right**), leaving any stones to sink to the bottom.*

If your clay is *wet* when found, you've saved a step and some time.
Just dig back into the vein a bit to get away from surface debris (this will
only have to be removed), then dig up the clay and put it into a vessel of
some sort for carrying.

If the clay you've found is dry, it needs to be rewetted. There are lots of ways to do this.

What most "good" potters do is to pound or grind up the clay before adding water (to allow for better absorption). They then add enough water to completely dissolve the particles and to make a "slurry" solution. You want it *kinda* thin—the purpose being to allow you to stir the solution well. Let it set for 20 to 30 seconds (allowing the heavier stones and so on to settle), and then carefully pour off the thinner, silty clay solution into another container. This can be repeated if necessary. Once almost all the impurities seem to be removed, set the container aside, allowing the heavier clay to settle and occasionally pouring off the lighter water. This can take several days. As the clay begins to thicken, you can spread it out on a smooth surface to speed the drying. When it reaches the right consistency, it's ready to use.

As the mixture is allowed to set, the clay settles and the water can be poured off. Using a rawhide container speeded this process, as moisture could evaporate through the skin.

Further drying is expedited by "pancaking" the clay.

Often when we're in a hurry to make a bowl (I'm always in a hurry, it seems!), we just mix water and clay, kneading and working it till it's "right," feeling the larger impurities and removing them with our fingers. This works well especially with smaller, quickie bowls when you're rushed. But it's believed that the longer the clay sits wet, the better it will be to work with.

For working, the moisture content must be just right. Too wet, and it'll be too sticky and will slump, not holding its shape. Too dry, and it will crack as you work it. If a little too wet, it can either be spread out to dry some or just worked in your hands, allowing the sun and breeze to dry it. This additional working is good for the clay, most notably for removing pockets of air. If the clay is only a bit dry, what works well is to dip your hands in water, shake off the excess, and then work the clay.

Not all clays will work in making containers, owing to their chemical compounds.

A good, simple test is to roll a handful of clay pencil-thin and tie it into a knot. If it doesn't break or crack, it's a good candidate. Plasticity is the key here.

The amount of shrinkage during drying is also an important factor. Too much can hurt. The addition of temper (see that section below) can sometimes help.

One clay that we've worked with a lot was touted by all who touched and worked with it as having a "great feel." Well, we've never yet gotten a good firing out of it. This was a clay that had all the outward characteristics of a good, usable clay—pliability, shrinkage, feel—but it just wouldn't hold up to firing. It blew apart.

So, if you follow all instructions and *still* have firing problems, change clays.

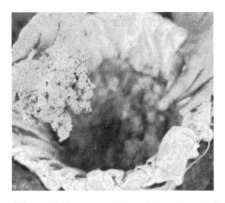

Clay with just enough moisture to wet. Let set for a short time and then work well with your hands, picking and cleaning.

An easy test to check for pliability.

Temper

To potters, *temper* means to mix (clay) with water or a modifier (such as grog). Grog is a collective term for refractory (resistant to heat) materials, such as crushed pottery and firebricks, used to make refractory products (as crucibles) that reduce shrinkage in drying and firing.

First we clean the clay of rubble. Then do we add more rubble to the clay?

We had a lot of questioning to do on this one, and found no single answer. Most consultants we spoke with agreed on several points, though none gave us a firm definition. Many admitted that they had no idea exactly what was happening here. Several had theories.

I'll list here what we've noted from others, and what we've also come up with ourselves:

- The temper (grog) is a stable.
- The clay is not.
- A lot of rubble (stones and so forth) in the fresh-dug clay is not a stable, so it needs to be removed.
- During drying, and especially during firing, the clay will shrink and expand to a certain degree. Here, a little goes a long way—too much action and the pot cracks or breaks. The temper helps to keep the vessel (clay) more stable during these periods.
- Some clays don't require temper. Others might need up to a one-third addition. As noted earlier, each clay has its own special properties.
- Small pots require less temper than larger ones, or sometimes none.
- Large pots tend to slump when building, but the addition of temper helps to counteract this.
- The intended use of the finished product has some bearing. Vessels that will be in and out of the fire (each time experiencing expansion and contraction) will require more temper than those used primarily for storage.
- The addition of temper actually weakens the pot. More and coarser temper should be added to cooking vessels, as it takes the heat shock better.

Geri thinks of temper as being the main ingredient and of clay as just holding it together—kinda like working cement. Steve Watts opines that, on a microscopic level, pottery begins to break down as soon as you start to use it. Minuscule cracks develop every time that the pot is heated or cooled. He strongly feels that the temper acts as a stopping point for these cracks, like drilling a hole in a windshield at the end of a crack to stop its progress.

Now that we've got some idea of just what temper is and the purpose thereof, what do we use as temper?

Sand and grit are usually readily available for temper purposes. But beware of what makes up the sand in your area. Where we live there must be some limestone in it, and our limestone isn't stable. Every time that we've used it, the pots have blown in firing. By contrast, limestone in the southeastern United States is different, and works.

Grass, dried cow dung, and other organic materials can be used.

Broken, fired pottery (shards), when crushed fine, can be reused.

Shell is often good. Most (perhaps all) shell will work. We've used freshwater mussel successfully. One caution, though: Fire or burn the shell first. Unfired shell isn't stable. The initial expansion when being fired is more than in clay, and firing stabilizes it. We've had some shell material, after "cooking" and firing, absorb moisture and swell in the pot, thereby breaking.

This list should cover most circumstances, so now let's put it all together and make something we can use in a wilderness situation.

Sand.

Pot shards to be used as temper.

Left: *Mussel shells being fired.*
Right: *The fired shell crumbles and is now stable.*

Construction

Mix the temper and clay to the desired proportions, then *don't stop:* Keep on working it. It can't be worked too much. Slam it. Beat it. Work it in your hands or on a hard surface. Compress everything well, and remove any and all air pockets. If a bit wet, work it till it dries just right. If dry, wet it by dipping your fingers in water. Once the "right" wetness is achieved, I find myself constantly rewetting by dipping fingers to keep it just right.

At some point, take a baseball-sized hunk of the mixture and work with that. Work it…work it…*work it.*

After several minutes, take the ball of clay and begin forcing your fist or fingers into it to develop a hollow—this is the beginning of the pot. Keep the forming pot moving in a circular fashion on the fist, meanwhile constantly beating, tapping, compressing the walls. Work out any cracks. Just keep working it—you'll begin to "feel" the clay.

Start "pulling" clay from the bottom up toward the top. Put your fingers against the inside walls of the pot and pat the outside opposite to further compress. (Here some folks use a smooth stone on the inside and a wooden "paddle" on the outside. The paddle's usually wrapped with cordage to help prevent sticking. The technique is called, appropriately, "paddling.") All air pockets need to be worked out, as ***they can explode in firing.***

In not too many minutes you'll find yourself with a smallish bowl literally on your hands.

At this point I'll run my slightly dampened fingers over the whole pot, inside and out, smoothing and compressing, all the while being careful not to get it too wet.

Now, if you have the pot the size that you want it (cereal-bowl size?), set it on a piece of bark or whatever's handy (making it easier to move around) and set it in the shade to dry *slowly*. Fast drying will have the tendency to crack the product. It will now take from a coupla days to a coupla weeks, depending on conditions, of slow drying. Keep it protected. *All* moisture needs to escape. It must be bone dry.

> **To repeat my caution: Any moisture left in the clay will explode in firing.**

Temper added to clay.

Mix well ...beat...

Chop...slap...

Pound...fist.

Beginning to form.

Pat to compress and then pull the clay up.

If you have too much clay, pinch a little off and continue to form.

Pinching, patting...

Rubbing, smoothing...

Before you know it, you have a bowl!

Set it aside in shade to slowly dry.

Now, if you want to create a larger pot, form it this way as big as you can before slumping occurs. When you reach a certain height, the pot will begin to sag or slump because of its own weight. You now have to let the main body of the pot dry somewhat before adding more weight, but you also need to keep the rim wet so that more clay can be "welded" to it.

Set the pot in the shade. Wet the rim with damp fingers, and cover with green leaves or something similar to keep the *rim* from drying too much as the body dries. This may take only an hour or so, or maybe overnight.

When the pot's ready for the addition of more clay, roll out a coil of prepared clay (called "coiling"), the same thickness as the pot walls (less than 1/4" and up to 1/2").

This now can be added to the pot. Be careful not to add too much weight at once. You may be able to apply more than one coil at a time. Just don't get too rushed. Use your fingernail or a tool of bone or wood or something else, to "draw" the coils together, both inside and out. Squeeze and compress it all together to weld into one. In this manner, you can build the pot about as large as you desire.

If you wish it larger, roll out a coil and add it on.

Pinch, compress, and pull it together.

Cover the fresh added clay with wet leaves to keep the rim from drying as the rest of the pot does.

When you're satisfied, set the pot aside, as you did with the smaller pot. It needs to be *bone dry*—but it must dry slowly. As mentioned earlier, this may take up to two weeks.

Well, not all rules are set in clay, so to speak. Maria-Louise Sidoroff made a large vessel one time, beginning with fresh clay in the morning and firing it that evening. She speeded up the drying process by rotating it around a fire. It worked! On several occasions while in the field we've dug clay and built pots one day, dried them (controlled) by the fire the next day, and fired them on the second or third day.

After a day or so, under most circumstances, the pots can be handled. We usually turn the pots upside down at some stage in the drying to allow the bottom to dry well.

If you'd like to decorate the pot (perhaps using cordage marks from a paddle, or rolling a corn cob over it), this should be done before drying. When the pot's still fresh, or after the initial drying of a day or so called "leather dry", lines can be etched into it. This *can* be done when dry but seems to work better at the leather-dry stage.

Leather dry is also the stage to thin the pot, if you wish, by gently scraping away thicker areas, using a piece of bone, stone, or shell.

A very smooth pebble or a piece of bone can be used to smooth and burnish the pot. This is a good idea for the inside of a pot designed for cooking or eating. This can be done at the leather-dry or dry stage.

So what do we have up till now? We've found a source of clay, dug it, cleaned it, dirtied it (added temper), carefully made a pot, designed it, and *slowly* dried it.

Still one more major step to go, and that's next.

If you want to use a bowl for food or drink, sanitize it by burnishing the inside with a smooth stone.

Burnish the outside, if desired, for decoration.

Firing

The last step in your pot making is the firing. What you've read in earlier sections concentrated all your efforts on building and drying. You were left to assume that if the pot made it through these stages, you had it made—*wrong!*

By just slapping some clay around, you can have success up to this stage, but you'll lose many pots through careless firing. Care must be taken!

In *primitive* firing (meaning without sophisticated equipment and gas-fired kilns), lots can go wrong, and the pots are highly susceptible to breakage at this stage. Some old-time primitive potters speak of a failure rate of up to 50 percent.

Actually, we should refer to the firing in two stages, the prefiring and the firing.

As the pot heats, it will expand, and any remaining moisture (*not all of it* leaves in the previous drying) has to be driven out, slowly. So we want to proceed slowly. Gradual heating throughout. So we preheat.

Then the pot must be transferred from indirect heat to direct heat. We lose a lot of them here.

Two other critical stages are, first, when the pot reaches a temperature of around the boiling point (212°F) and the remaining *unnatural* water leaves and, second, when the pot reaches a temperature of 800° to 900°F and the *natural* chemical water of the clay is burned out. After this second stage, the clay can't be returned to its original condition and be reworked.

When firing your pots, avoid windy or rain-threatening days. A cool draft or even a drop of rain can ruin your efforts.

Let's list some firing techniques and tips.

Firing Method #1

A simple method for firing an individual pot, which produces varying results, we once saw done by Evard Gibby of Idaho.

He simply scrapes a wide depression in the ground an inch or so deep and a coupla feet in diameter. In there he puts some small rocks, on which to place the overturned pot. Then he sets a length of cordwood about the same diameter as the pot is high on either side of it, leaving a small space between log and pot. Then he places two more pieces of same-sized wood between the ends of the first two, up to and almost touching the pot. Next he crumbles cow chips (dried manure) to cover the pot and then covers it all with smaller pieces of wood. Finally, he builds a larger pile of wood (tipi shaped) over this, and lets the whole thing burn. He takes care to let the pot cool slowly.

We've done some firings like this in the past, and have had varying success with our own clay.

*Surrounding with logs (**left**) and covering with dried cow manure (**right**).*

Covering with more sticks and building into a tipi fire.

Touch it off.

The end result.

That's it. One step (no preheating). We can vouch for the fact that it's successful, for small pots at least.

In other firing methods, the pot must first be preheated.

Firing Method #2

Some people build a circular fire around pots and gradually move the fire in till finally the pots are actually resting in the fire itself. They eventually build the fire up with larger pieces of wood and let it burn for a coupla hours. Or, instead of using large pieces of wood, they constantly replenish it with smaller twigs spaced around, between, and above the pots.

Preheat.

Set on coals a bit and then gradually move the fire in.

Get it closer, higher, and hotter—finally, build it over.

Firing Method #3

Another method is to build a fire and to move the pot (or pots) closer, turning and rotating them till well preheated, then scraping the fire away and laying the pots in the coals or ashes or on an insulated layer of preheated rocks or old pottery shards. Let the pots sit a short time to allow gradual heating up before adding more fire.

Firing Method #4

From Steve Watts comes a technique for "firing the Catawba way," as he calls it. Preheat. Set on coals for a bit, then add pine needles, and so forth, to make for a slow heating. Then begin adding small woods, and then finally larger woods. When burned to coals, rebuild. Do twice for small pots. Three times for larger ones.

Firing Method #5

Over the years we've settled on one method that gives us 100 percent success…most times. We came to this through trial and error, because the clay that we've had the most success with here is touchy and fails when we fire using other methods. It's pretty much the same as a method described earlier, with a few changes. To make a fire in a ring, the easiest way we've found is by first building a fire to preheat the ground and then, when it burns down, raking the coals and small embers out into the size circle needed.

Building a circle fire is next to impossible. But making a circle fire as described is easy! Once circled, place small, stable (unblowupable: my word) stones or pieces of brick to put the pots on, place the pots on the stones (we almost always place them top down to keep hot coals from failing inside and adding too much heat too soon), and build up the ring of fire. Keep enough distance from fire to nearest pots so that you don't heat too fast, with more distance on the upwind side. Keep the fire alive and move it slowly toward the pots, ensuring that the heating is gradual. More and bigger fire. Closer and closer.

When a few inches from the fire's actually touching the pots (remember, upwind will be a longer distance), build the fire high enough so that long sticks can be placed on top of the fire to make a roof a few inches above the pots. Things go fast at this point. What you're doing is almost making a kiln with the fire. The cooler air from outside the ring will sweep the flames and heat into the center and up. You must keep the actual flames from most direct contact with the pots (for now), but much heat is applied.

Finally, you're putting a roof over it all, which will create more heat from above. We've found that this method makes for a more-even heating of the pots at a critical stage, allowing them to get a lot hotter before having the flames totally consume them. It takes about 1 1/2 to 2 hours, on a perfect day with no excess winds, and a whole lot of wood, resulting in a close to 100 percent success rate.

One disadvantage in placing the pots upside down is that, if there's any moisture in the ground, the steam created will rise into the pots with nowhere to go. This can cause cracks and possibly breakage.

Firing Method #6

One more firing method, which we haven't found in common use in the States, is the use of a *primitive* kiln (hardening oven). This gives you more control in heating gradually. Simply, the kiln is dug into a hillside, with a firing chamber below it. The heat and smoke from the fire is tunneled through the kiln. The ancient Chinese used this extensively, often stair-stepping kilns up a hillside, heating from a single fire chamber. You must ensure that the firing chamber is of sufficient size to heat the kiln to the required temperature (1200° to 1600°F; the color will be from dark red at the lower temperature through cherry red, bright cherry red, and orange at the higher temperature). This temperature should be maintained for two to four hours. The chimney escape should ideally be through the bottom of the kiln (so as to retain as much heat as possible—heat rises, remember?) and then up (see drawing on next page). The opening needs to be large enough to allow sufficient draw for the fire to reach the high temperatures required.

I think that this shows you that firing pottery just ain't throwing pots into the fire—though it's not all that difficult, either.

Last Words

Pots are made to use, so use 'em. The final test is to cook in them. Try to remember the word "gradual." Cold water in a hot pot can be disastrous. Same vice versa. Heat with coals or small flames.

When handling hot pots, use leather pot holders or wooden "tongs." Cloth can burst into flames.

Avoid lifting a pot by its rim, as you just might break it off.

Advice from Maria-Louise Sidoroff, whose expertise in making and using primitive pottery is known internationally: "A well constructed and sound pot will get better with usage. Using ordinary precautions, the life expectancy would be many, many years."

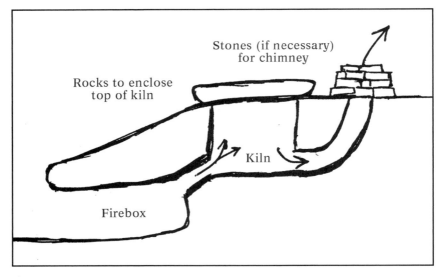

Stones (if necessary) for chimney

Rocks to enclose top of kiln

Kiln

Firebox

🌿 *Kiln can be lined with rocks.*

🌿 *Pots should be set on rock pillars.*

🌿 *Have removable rock at lid for use as peephole to check pots' color (temperature).*

The final test—using your pot.

Notes on Aboriginal Pottery

by Steve Watts (1989)

To me, the pottery trip is divided into three parts:

1/3 is making it (Good clay, well prepared, proper temper, and good construction techniques)

1/3 is firing it (Proper prefiring, and a thorough high firing with adequate cool-down time)

1/3 is using it (Proper care and use for storage, cooking, and so on)

After all, using pottery is the main purpose for making it. For a pot to be functional, it must be well made. In other, obvious words—the better a pot is constructed and fired, the better it will operate as a cooking vessel.

On a microscopic level, pottery starts to break down as soon as you start to use it. But a well-made pot will last through many cookings if taken care of and treated properly.

Pots should be stored in a secure spot, properly supported, and protected from running children, dogs, and the like.

An underfired pot (in whole or in part) will fall apart when first used—literally dissolve. Many pots only made for display fall into this underfired category.

Of course shock must be avoided—putting cold water into a hot pot or vice versa.

Some folks suggest filling the pot with water prior to use and letting it stand in the pot long enough to thoroughly saturate the walls before using. Others have suggested preheating and oiling the pot to season it, à la cast iron.

Both of the procedures are probably useful, but my experience is that with a well-made pot one simply adds "room temperature" water plus the food to be cooked to the unheated pot and sets it on the fire. Stoke up the flames and cook away.

Chapter 10

Brain-Tan Buckskin

I first attempted brain tanning 1974. At that time I could locate few sources pertaining to this subject. What I did come up with left a lot to be desired. My results were unsuccessful, but enough small bits of the skin did work out to give me hope and show me what could be accomplished if done properly. (I had no idea at that time what real buckskin was even like. I had read only vague references to Indian-tanned skins.) All of what I could find on this subject was written by someone who had no hands-on experience but was writing what had been observed or heard. That may not be a bad way to describe a procedure, but it's hardly the way to write a "how-to."

With more and more interest shown in going back to basics since then, and especially the blossoming interest in buckskinning, more has been written about some of the natural and primitive ways and skills. I sure haven't had the opportunity to read all that has been written on brain tanning, and probably don't know the existence of even half of it. From what I've read, however, combined with my personal recent experiences of trying to learn more about it, I feel that I've done a lot better than the others.

Most of what I've read, if read by someone not at all familiar with the procedure (and, to my way of thinking, "how-to" books and articles should be addressed to those who don't know "how to"), leaves the reader with a lot of questions unanswered. If read with no other purpose than the joy of reading or to further one's knowledge somewhat, fine. But most such texts don't work for the individual interested in taking a raw deerskin and turning it into a fine piece of material, especially if that individual hardly knows what a deer is.

This chapter was written to deliberately oversimplify, because *brain tanning just isn't as difficult as most accounts tend to make it appear*. But I don't belittle the amount of effort required, when I demonstrate that a skin can be finished in as little as nine hours—given ideal working conditions. Of course, many, many variables can and do affect the quality of the finished product.

It's frustrating and time-consuming to have to search out numerous sources to learn a new skill. I've tried to make this chapter as complete and easy to follow as what I wanted and needed when I did my first skin. I've had my drafts read by uninformed people, both male and female, and tried to incorporate their suggestions for clarity. I want this chapter to work. It was designed so that the interested and motivated person with no foreknowledge at all in skins could take this chapter, a raw deerskin, and very minimal materials and end up with a finished buckskin. I'm satisfied that it will do that.

I strongly suggest that you read this chapter carefully. Study the photographs, reread, learn what's happening to the skin and why. Go over the various steps till you know what each is accomplishing. Some parts of this may seem complicated on the first reading, but if you study it closely you'll find that I've made things easier and faster for you, such as lacing into the frame. You can lace it any damn way that you want (and for one skin maybe you should). But I feel certain that when you find out how simply and quickly you can make buckskin, you won't stop at a single skin.

I speak throughout of the average 10-square-foot deerskin, which is a large skin. Actually, the deer we have in north central Kansas average larger than that. Smaller skins, of course, will require less time and effort.

I have purposely not gone into the making of anything but buckskin, so as to keep things as simple as possible. You'll find nothing here about working larger hides or furs. The basic principles are the same, but there are certain differences for each. As with anything worthwhile, it will take some effort and sweat, but not nearly what most have been led to believe. There's no secret here—only simple rules.

Brief, All-Important Summary

Pay attention. What I describe here may not actually be the scientific facts that some are searching for, but if you understand what's put forth here you'll know what's happening to the skin, and why. This knowledge not only will help you to better approach the task at hand, but also will be invaluable in troubleshooting and correcting mistakes.

First you must understand the product that you're working with—the skin.

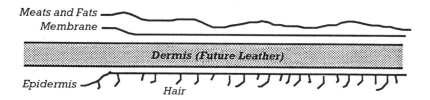

The future leather (the dermis) actually consists of millions of tiny threads. You *must* visualize this. Think of it as highly compressed cotton. An inherent property of these threads is glue. Boil them down and you have hide glue. Oils, in our case from the brains of the deer (10W motor oil might work, and Ivory soap does too, but not as well as brains), are penetrated *completely* through the dermis to coat all these threads. In the methods illustrated here, the brains (oils) are mixed with water. Water is thinner than the oils and therefore penetrates easier, drawing the oils with it. But the *oils won't penetrate through the membranes*, sandwiching either side of the skin. Water will. Oils won't. Thus the necessity of removing these membranes. The inner membrane, which is a solid sheet, is easily removed, most times done completely while fleshing. Sandpaper will show where this has been missed. The outer membrane, the epidermis, is neither harder nor more or less important to remove than the inner, but it's the *hardest for you to learn to remove*. The epidermis is not a solid sheet. In fact, it compares to sandpaper, with millions of tiny dots making up the grain of leather. The epidermis is removed, in our method, by dry scraping, or removing the hair and the epidermis at the same time. Your scraper will remove hair *and* epidermis from an area about 1/4" at a lick. Work an area about 1" wide, overlap your strokes, let your eyes penetrate into the skin—you'll eventually see what you're removing. It does *not* look the same all over the skin. It may take 10 to 12 strokes before you've successfully removed the epidermis from your 1" inch wide strip. Pay attention.

Once the surfaces are prepared, the oils will be able to penetrate. We need to coat *every* fiber with these oils, hence the repeated applications. You can't overbrain. But, once oiled, if left unattended, the skin will shrink and dry hard (the glue taking effect). If you move these lubricated fibers on themselves while the skin dries, the oils will allow the fibers to stay separated and they'll swell somewhat. The result: unbelievably soft, flannel-like leather.

But if this was to be wetted, the fibers would again shrink and dry hard (the glue) unless worked. If instead we penetrate the entire, loosely woven skin with smoke, the pitch from the smoke will *waterproof the fibers*. The skin itself isn't waterproofed. Water will run through it. But the fibers will be waterproofed, and the wetted skins will again dry soft since the water hasn't been allowed to get to the individual fiber and allow the glue to take effect.

Once you understand this, you're in control.

(I became aware of the glue action mentioned above through Jim Rigg's book *Blue Mountain Buckskin*—the importance of always learning.)

Now, a note pertaining to finishing the skin out. I describe herein finishing it out by pulling over a rope, or also by hand. Many, many others accomplish the same by a method described as "staking." This means, after braining, lacing the skin back onto the frame and working the fibers by applying force with a rounded stick.

I think of the skin, stretched on the frame after fleshing, as being stretched 100 percent. When the skin has been cut from the frame and, after braining, has been worked by hand, *it will shrink about 20 percent*. When staked, the skin will stretch another 5 to 10 percent to its limits.

On the one hand, you end up with a larger skin. On the other, the skin, though 25 to 30 percent smaller, is also that much thicker, and spongier, and stretchier. To me it is alive yet.

One advantage to working the skin by hand: At any time it can be rolled up, placed in a plastic bag, and frozen till such time as you want to get back to it. Once you begin staking, though, you'll have to stake till you're done.

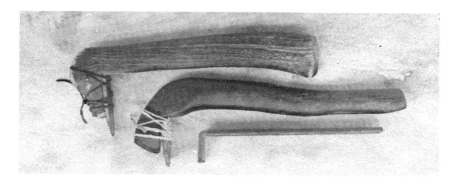

The only tool necessary to end up with buckskin.
Top: *Elk antler handle with steel blade.*
Middle: *Wooden Osage orange handle with flint blade.*
Bottom: *Steel handle.*

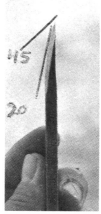

Left: *Front view of file blade. Roundness prevents tearing into skin.*

Right: *Side view; extreme angle is put on with grinder at approximately 20–25°—working angle of approximately 45° is put on with whetstone (line).*

A Simple Breakdown

Day 1

	STEP	HOURS
6:30–8 a.m.	Frame and flesh	1 1/2
12–12:30 p.m.	Prepare flesh side	1/2
3–4:30 p.m.	Dehair	1 1/2
4:30–5 p.m.	Prepare hair side	1/2
5–6:15 p.m.	Prepare and apply brains	1 1/4
6:15–6:45 p.m.	Stretch skin open and wrap in towels/refrigerate	1/2
Day 2		
8–11 a.m.	Finish stretching	3
TOTAL HOURS		8 3/4

During the afternoon of Day 2 the skin could be smoked. This simplified schedule is figuring ideal weather for drying.

Materials

A big advantage of tanning (dressing) your skins with brains is the minimum of expenditure required for materials. Most materials, if not all, will be on hand in the average home.

Knife—Useful for making lacing holes. A pocket or paring knife is all that's necessary. The only requirements are a thin, sharp blade and a good point.

Four **2x4s** about 8' long, and **nails.** Cedar or pine poles lashed or nailed securely, or both, will work fine. It must be a good, solid frame.

125–150' of **1/8" nylon cord** in 25–30'. lengths, or whatever else you come up with. Nylon is easy to work with, and long-lasting.

Sandpaper—#50 coarse grit works well for medium and larger skins. Use a finer grit for smaller, thinner skins.

Brains—I've heard tell of others using liver, pancreas, and other oily organs. I have never used anything but brains. The brain from the critter was used "back then." Mine comes packaged neatly in 1 lb. plastic containers from the local supermarket. Get yours where you can.

Bucket—Something in the 2- to 3-gallon size is convenient. Material doesn't matter.

A **wringer** from an old wringer washer. Certainly not very primitive or natural but sure does work well. (The stick is the natural way.)

About 15–20' of good, tight, **heavy rope.** The best I've found is a lariat. Definitely something that won't unravel as you rub the skin back and forth across it, and at least 1/2" in diameter.

Scraper—To work their skins and hides, the Indians used a section of elk antler with either a flint or, in later times, a steel blade attached. I used an antler once and found it ideal. With no access to elk antlers in northeast Kansas, I use the next best, Osage orange. Any hardwood will suffice, the heavier the better.

Scraper: Handle from Osage orange, blade from a file.

I used a dead piece of wood about 2" in diameter and 18" long with a limb protruding at a 90° angle at one end. After debarking, scraping, and sanding smooth, I sawed into the knot at a 90° angle, creating a platform on which to tie the blade. The blade was made from a section of old file (any hard steel will work; a file is usually handy) about 3" long, rounded on one end and with an edge applied at a 45° angle. I tied the file to the handle and was ready to go.

The first two skins I did were done with a well-rounded, heavy skinning knife. I finished several using a hog scraper, well rounded. I've even used an old hand-held flint scraper I found in a campsite.

Not all skins need to be extra-large No. 1. This small "Bambi" with large cut still made a nice, 6 sq. ft. skin.

Skins

Acquiring deerskins really isn't that difficult. There are many sources from which you may obtain them if you look and ask around. During deer season I can acquire 15 to 20 from friends and acquaintances who have no use for them. There are also a number of locker plants in the area that will sell me as many as I want at the going rate—sometimes as little as $2, but normally closer to $5. Contact with local law and game enforcement officers also informs me of many road kills.

Wherever you get your skins, some words of caution. Most hunters who skin their own, and all butchers whom I've run across, take great pride in how fast they can remove the skin from the deer. The quicker and the cleaner that the skin is removed does no favors for the tanner but only leaves numerous holes and "scores" (cuts into the skins not deep enough to be holes—yet).

When I skin a deer it takes me from 15 to 30 minutes to do the job, depending on whether it's done in the field or from the front-end loader of a tractor. When the skin is to be tanned I'm not a fast skinner; I am *careful*. The knife is used sparingly, and I leave all stubborn bits of meat and fat on the skin. They come off easily enough later, with no appreciable loss of meat to the hunter. By being a bit more careful I don't end up with a skin full of holes or, worse yet, the many, many scores that can take a good No. 1 skin and turn it into a piece of crap. Light scores on the thicker part of the skin, such as the neck, are usually acceptable, but the normal score on the average part of the skin will, 9 times out of 10, tear out while you're working the skin in the final stretching process. *Beware of scores!*

To collect as many good skins as possible, I may offer to skin them out for local hunters, who are usually pleased as punch to have me do this for them, especially when it's as cold as it can get around here in December. As an added bonus I'm almost always allowed to remove the loin sinew strips also.

As for getting skins from the butcher, well, you often have to take what you can get. Just before deer season I always go around to the processors with whom I've made arrangements and ask them to please use the knife sparingly. This usually helps.

There are three common ways to keep the skins till you're ready to tan them. The oldest way is to just leave them exposed to the air till they're dry. This is also the most time-consuming later, as they must be soaked in fresh water for what seems like forever to make them as soft and pliable as when green.

Salting the skin for preservation is the second method, and probably the most commonly used. The flesh side is coated liberally with salt and the excess moisture allowed to drain off. It will keep this way for six to eight months before needing to be resalted. Although it most assuredly works, I don't use this method myself, as it requires a lot of time and water to wash out the salt, all of which must be removed. Salt draws moisture. Unsmoked brain tan dries stiff if moistened.

By far the easiest way to keep them is the third way: frozen. I freeze a skin as soon after collecting it as I can, by rolling it (hair side out); tying it in a tight, neat bundle; and placing it in an airtight plastic bag. I'm now tanning skins that have been frozen this way for up to three years. I believe that they could be kept forever this way and still be as green and fresh when thawed as the day they were put up, though you need to keep air away from the flesh side. By keeping the skin frozen I eliminate any need to wash or soak the skin before tanning, which saves considerable time, energy, and water. Only the bloodiest of skins will I even wash. The skin will dry quite a bit faster and be ready to work sooner if the hair isn't moistened.

Framing and Fleshing

Now let's do something with that skin, wherever it came from.

If it was dried, then you'd best find a source of running water, such as a stream, and weight the skin with rocks and leave it for a couple of days or so. It will take a long time to get it back to the same state it was in when taken from the deer. You do need to check it every so often to ensure that the fresh water is getting to the entire skin. If you don't have access to a creek or a stream, place it into a large container, such as a 25-gallon trash can, and soak. The water must be changed regularly, after only several hours the first few times, and probably at least every 10 to 12 hours from then on till it's workable. On warmer days be sure that the water doesn't heat enough to rot the skin. It needs to soak till as pliable and fresh as when removed from the deer.

A salted skin is more easily prepared. It needs only repeated washings to remove *all* the salt.

Frozen skins need only to be thawed.

When ready, roll the skin out on a level surface and trim the perimeter to remove all rough edges, including the lower legs. The skin can, of course, be tanned with the legs on but it adds a good deal of work. Right now let's get you proficient at making buckskin. You can do any extras later, after you master the basics.

When the skin is trimmed, stretch it to its natural shape and lay the 2x4s around it, nailing them together, two nails per corner. We want to build the frame about 8" to 10" larger on all sides of the skin, as the skin stretches quite a bit while being fleshed. While nailing the frame together, fold the skin on itself to prevent it from drying. You'll probably want to apply water to the flesh side at intervals to keep it fresh till you're finished fleshing.

Now to lace the skin to the frame: Place it on the ground or work table, flesh side up, and punch holes around the entire perimeter of the skin with a thin-bladed knife. The holes are to be 1/2" to 1" from the edge and approximately 1 1/2" to 3" apart. The easiest way to make these holes is to

Upper left: Frame built around skins.
Upper right: Laced on three sides.
Lower: Completely laced.

place a board under the skin, push the point of the knife against the skin into the board with one hand, and pull the skin up with the other. I say to use a *thin* blade, because you don't want the holes too large.

To keep the natural shape of the skin square within the frame as you lace, I've found it convenient to tie each corner of the skin to the corresponding corner of the frame with a 12" to 15" cord. Also, place the skin just a little off center to the right (as you face it from the bottom). After having done a few skins, you'll find no need to tie the corners in order to square it within the frame, though doing so sure helps the beginner.

Picture the frame in an upright position with the neck at the top and the flesh side facing you. You'll begin lacing at the neck at the upper left corner. From that corner, go through the hole at the corner of the neck, out under the 2x4, and in over it again to the skin. Now begin to take the cord through three holes at a time as if you were sewing—the cord, as it passes through the series of three holes, runs in and out in a straight line, not wrapped around the edge. Then take the cord out under the frame and in over it, and then do three more holes. The cord always comes from the skin out under the frame and back over it to the skin. I normally go through three holes at a lick, sometimes two and very seldom four, but only as long as the holes are in a straight line. This is to save the inconvenience of having to replace if one of the holes rips out. As the edge of the skin turns at legs and corners, bring your cord around the frame and begin your series of holes again. At the neck where the skin's the thickest, I'll go through only one hole if that's the way the count ends up at the corner.

Don't pull the cord too tightly but just "snug it up" for now. When you reach the end of one length of cord, tie it off and begin with another. I normally leave two or three holes (one series) for the rope that I tied off to go through as I take up the slack. As you round the second corner and begin the bottom, you can begin to take up some of the slack—but not too tight now or you'll lose the shape. (Never pull too tightly on the bottom, as it will easily tear.) After you go around the third corner and into the home stretch, you can really begin to tighten things up, even going back to the bottom section and taking up the remainder of the slack there. By the time you reach the neck, whence you began, the skin will be fairly taut and close to being centered on the frame.

If the skin seems to dry some while the lacing process is going on, simply splash water on it to keep it wet. For now you want the skin kept fresh and pliable.

Now stand the frame, neck up, against a tree or the side of a shed. It's best to keep the skin in the shade at this stage to keep it from drying too fast as you flesh. It's also a good idea to always keep the frame tied to a tree or structure so that a sudden gust of wind doesn't send it flying. Now, beginning at the neck, tighten the ropes all around the skin till it's as tight as a drum on the frame. You'll have to retighten these as you flesh, for the skin will stretch considerably.

Taking the scraper (I like it very sharp, but you must be extremely careful not to cut into the skin itself), begin at the neck and remove every bit of the meat, fat, and membrane that you possibly can. The knife will come in handy here at certain spots, such as around the legs and along the edges. With some skins, this will be an easy job. With others, such as the old-timer trophy buck, your work will be cut out for you. You may be tempted on some of these heavier skins to leave quite a bit on till the next step, but believe me, now's the time to remove it. It's damn near impossible to remove all the membrane at this point, but get what you can. Definitely get all the meat and fat off.

Flesh, fats, and membrane are easily removed with scraper.

Don't attempt to clean all the way to the edge, or you'll end up cutting the cords or ripping out the holes, or both. The perimeter is cut off later and discarded.

Keep the skin tight within the frame. This way it fleshes much more easily than a loose, sloppy one, plus you have a lot less chance of accidentally cutting into it with the scraper.

Neck and right side fleshed clean. Note remaining layer of flesh on left side. All must be removed.

Once the skin is as clean as you can get it, leave it and go on to something else for a while. You can do nothing further with it till it's completely dry. With the high humidity here in northeast Kansas, that can take from six to eight hours on a good day. Drier climates will, of course, make drying a lot faster.

Surface Preparation

When the stretched skin has dried *completely*, both sides must now be prepared so that the brain matter will be allowed to penetrate completely into the thickest areas.

I've read and heard that the skin shouldn't be allowed to dry in the sun, for various reasons. Many times I've left my skins in full sun to help speed the drying process and have found that it makes no difference whatsoever in the working of the product or its finished condition. It does cause some curling of the skin because of uneven drying, but that hasn't yet interfered in my working of it. The hair side will naturally take longer to dry completely to the roots and epidermis, so if you're eager to proceed you might fluff the hair occasionally with a brush.

Leveling high spot of score with very sharp scraper.

Figuring that you're anxiously awaiting the skin to dry enough so as to continue the operation, begin with the flesh side when it's *good and dry*. This will be about midway to when the hair side is ready. Start with the *sharp* scraper and work *lightly* around the neck area down to the shoulders and all the way around the perimeter of the skin. These are the areas where you most likely left on some of the membrane, which must be completely removed for the brain to penetrate into the skin itself. (Water, being a liquid, will penetrate this. Brain and its accompanying oils are thicker and won't penetrate through this membrane, nor through the epidermis on the other side.)

Carefully work the scraper around the rough high areas of any scores, in the direction that they lie—never across them—to even these areas off. Also, carefully work the scraper around any holes.

Membrane on flesh side.

Now take sandpaper and go over every inch of the surface to remove any small bits of membrane and to level the surface. This will also have the added benefit of "bringing up the nap," which will allow better absorbency of the brain. Sand the neck area first and then do a strip around the entire perimeter several inches wide. Divide the remainder into quarters and sand them one at a time till you're positive that every square inch has been covered. This method helps to ensure that every last bit is clean and smooth. Missing even as little as one small area can result in a rough, stiff spot.

Start the sanding with long strokes, using a block, and finish off by

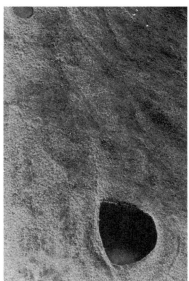

Flesh side. **Left:** *Fleshed and dried.*
Right: *High areas scraped and sanded, ready for brain.*

using the sandpaper in your hand so that isolated, deliberate finger pressure can be applied where necessary. When finished, most of the surface will be soft and fluffy. This side is now ready for the application of the brain, but, of course, you'll need to work the other side first. (A fur would now be ready, but there are some different rules to follow with fur, which we won't delve into here. In this book we're sticking to the making of buckskin.) Tanning with hair on is covered in depth in our book *Primitive Wilderness Skills, Applied and Advanced.*

To prepare the hair side, take the very sharp scraper and begin at the neck to scrape the hair off. With a heavy, sharp scraper, this isn't much of a chore. First, clean a strip across the top of the skin (neck). Now with long, powerful downward strokes of the scraper, the hair will readily come off. You'll need to sharpen the blade several times during this process, as you want it really sharp. At the legs and at the flanks the hair lies in different directions and you'll have to scrape in different directions to get it to come off easily. For most of the body of the skin, what works best are good, powerful, downward strokes. Apply less pressure around the legs and at the flanks. It's wise to leave the flanks till last and then scrape them with a freshly sharpened blade, applying as little pressure as needed. Should you happen to "pop" a hole then, it won't interfere with the scraping of the rest of the skin. It's tricky to remove the hair from around one of these holes that just seem to pop up.

It's wise to mark any existing holes already in the skin before you begin,

First strip of hair scraped across top. Note hanging cords marking holes.

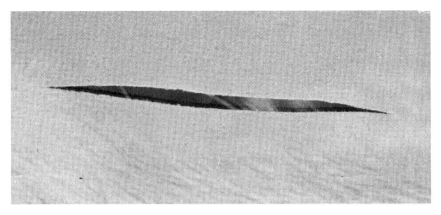

Cut caused by use of too-coarse sandpaper.

because the hair hides them completely. Do this by running a piece of rope or a small stick through each, which can be readily seen as you're dehairing. It's easy to forget they're there, and while energetically scraping away you may hit one of these holes and rip the skin, sometimes damn near in two. That's a sure way to take the thrill out of working skins. It can ruin your whole day, believe me.

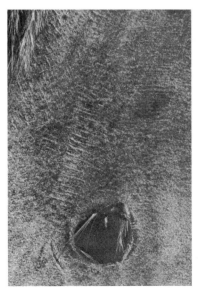
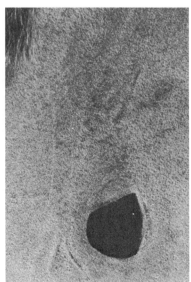

Left: *Hair side dehaired.*
Right: *Sanded and ready.*

When I get to dehairing, I move at a pretty fast pace, but *I watch each and every stroke of the scraper.* The hair comes off easily. The epidermis, which must also be removed (to allow the brains to penetrate), isn't always as easy to remove. Scrape every inch of the skin till you're certain that all the epidermis is off (very seldom is it ever entirely removed). If you closely study the skin as you go, you'll be able to see the epidermis. It isn't a solid sheet like the membrane on the flesh side, but more like a sandpaper coating. Although it can be seen on any part of the skin, it's most apparent at the flanks and other thinner areas. If the epidermis contains *any* moisture at all, it will be nearly impossible to remove. The areas where the hair is the thickest (such as the forward part of the flanks and the butt end) will be the last parts of the skin to dry completely. In these areas I've been known to scrape *very lightly with an extremely sharp blade* to remove the hair only, going back later to remove the epidermis with either the scraper or sandpaper. Damp epidermis is rubbery. It won't "work." You'll only tear the skin if you try.

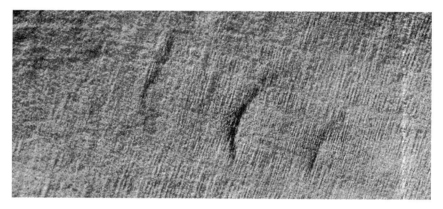

Three scores seen from hair side, ready for sanding.

When finished with the dehairing, I've been over every square inch of the skin. I *know* that the epidermis is removed and that any ridges created while scraping have been smoothed with the scraper. Now go over the entire surface with sandpaper as done on the other side. **Caution:** It's possible to sand completely through a skin, so go tenderly at thinner areas. Sometimes at the flanks, but especially at the scores, it may be best to leave some of the epidermis, going over it lightly with sandpaper only to break it up enough for the brains to penetrate. You'll have to feel a lot of this out and just do what seems right.

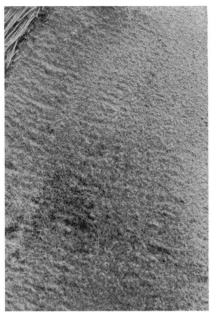

Hair side at flank. **Left:** *Note remaining epidermis.*
Right: *Skin is sanded and ready for brain.*

Braining

What needs to be done now is to get the oils of the brain into every pore
and fiber of the skin. This is the easiest and fastest step of the operation.

The primary sources of brain (if not from the critter we've taken the
skin from) are slaughterhouses, butchers, or the local market. I find it most
convenient to purchase brain by the pound, packed in your basic primitive
plastic container, from the local supermarket. They cost a bit more than a
coupla bucks per pound, and one pound is plenty enough to do one skin.
You shouldn't use less than a pound, as it needs to be mixed with a certain
volume of water.

Take your pound of brain and beat it thoroughly with an egg beater or
whirl in a blender. Add just a little water, maybe a cup, and beat away. You
can get by just squishing it with your hands. The object is to liquefy the brain
as much as possible. Now add this to approximately 3/4 to 1 gallon of water,
bring to a boil, and simmer till grayish white, about 10 to 15 minutes. Let
this cool till just comfortably warm to the touch.

With a large paintbrush or clean sponge, apply this solution to both sides of the skin. You don't need to be too liberal with the brain solution now. You just need to get the skin pliable enough to cut from the frame and fold easily into the bucket. Fold the now-pliable skin into the bucket of brain solution and work it with your hands for several minutes. With some of the smallest, thinnest skins, that's all that's necessary. But I've never yet let any skin get by with only one soaking in the brains. I've had too many skins not receive a deep enough penetration of the brain, which won't be discovered till I've spent several hours working the skin and suddenly wind up with a stiff product—and then have to return to this stage. That's a lot of extra work that can be easily prevented with very little effort now. There's no special time limit that the skin has to be left soaking in the brain. Once you've got complete penetration, you're ready to finish it out. The shortest time for small skins would be about 15 to 20 minutes, with two soakings.

With some of the thicker, larger skins, it works well to apply several coats of the brain before cutting from the frame. Each coat should be allowed to dry, preferably in the sun, and then either scraped or sanded before you apply the next coat.

Between soakings the skin must be wrung to remove as much moisture as possible. As mentioned before, the skin will absorb water like a sponge. Brain being a solid matter, and its oils being thicker than water, the liquefied brain won't be absorbed into the skin as readily as plain water. With the thinner areas, this is no problem, and one soaking is enough. The thicker area, though, will require additional soakings. You must get all the water out of the skin that you possibly can, so that when it's reimmersed into the solution the water not only will bring more brain with it but also will draw ever deeper what's already there.

The wringer from an old wringer washer works just fine for this. Run the skin through this several times.

The traditional way of wringing out excess water, and the way that I did all my skins till I found the wringer, is to drape the skin around a small tree limb (or a lariat stretched tightly), overlapping it by about one third of itself, and rolling and folding the skin onto and into itself, tucking in all loose ends till it's tightly rolled together. The accompanying photos show this better than I could hope to describe it. Place a solid stick (approximately 1" in diameter) through the opening and twist the skin till tight, pull, twist some more, and then pull some more. The moisture will run and drip out (place the bucket to catch the drippings). This will take only a few minutes. Now stretch the skin as open as you can get it, and repeat. After the second wringing, open and stretch the skin over the rope to really open the fibers up as much as possible. Pull in all directions. This will allow the brain better penetration on reimmersion. Return the skin to the solution. Repeat this process till you're certain of complete penetration. The average 10 sq. ft. skin should be put through this process four or five times. *You can't get too* much *brain into the skin, but you may not get* enough. After the final braining, wring the skin a few extra times to remove all possible moisture.

You'll find that this is the only stage in the process that actually attracts flies. If a fresh skin is used, the fleshing process isn't smelly, but flies sure are attracted to the brain.

Above left: *Wringing excess moisture from skin by hand before...*

(above middle) *putting it around rope and overlapping by about one third.*

Above right: *Rolling it into itself and (**below right**) inserting stick and twisting.*

Wringing out every bit of moisture.

Sewing of Holes

Holes. Every skin has a hole...or two...or three...or more. Some big, some little, and now's the time to do something about them. On occasion I've waited till finished with the tanning but then ended up with patches, which don't look all that bad but are more trouble and more time-consuming than what we'll do now. At this point I use artificial sinew for the thread. Later, when I finish the skin out, I redo the patches with real sinew. Any strong thread will work at this stage, but it must be strong enough to withstand the stretching and rubbing that the skin will endure from now on.

Most holes, except bullet holes, will lie in some particular direction. Sew them in the direction that they lie. Whip stitch the hole shut and tie off twice. The skin will be abused from now on, so make them good, tight stitches.

Poorly sewn holes will tear out, and weak thread will break. In addition to all holes, sew the thinner scores shut, as they too will invariably tear. Do all the sewing from the former flesh side, because the hair side will be used as the outside of any finished product.

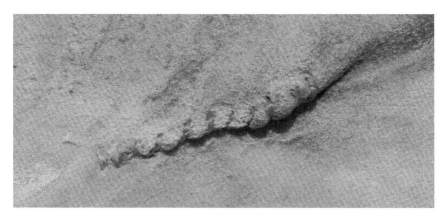

Hole sewn before finishing. Puckers will be eliminated while stretching.

Most skins have some form of scar tissue from old wounds. The most common are the long "scrapes" running down the center of the back, made when the animal goes under barbed wire fences. Scrape these a little with the small blade of a knife. Sometimes you can get rid of them, sometimes not.

You'll also often find larger areas of scar tissue, a result of a more serious wound to the deer in the past. Cut them out now and sew the hole shut. If these don't completely tear out as the skin's worked, they'll dry hard. A single seam shows less and is easier to do than a patch. After the stretching and working of the skin that follows, all puckers now visible will be eliminated. You can leave the holes sewn as is when finished, though often there will be stiffness where the stitches are. I resew with sinew. Usually the hole will have to be elongated slightly when this is done, to eliminate the pucker.

If there are many holes that require considerable time to sew, the edges of the skin may begin to dry too much and stiffen and you may need to add more moisture. This normally can be accomplished simply by wringing it one more time, to disperse the moisture already in the skin.

Many times at this point, if I want to delay the next step, I'll only stretch the skin once completely around to open the pores and then roll it in towels (to absorb moisture), seal it tightly in a plastic bag, and put it in either the fridge or the freezer. It can be left for several days like this in the refrigerator, or indefinitely in the freezer. If left too long in the refrigerator it'll sour and rot. The freezer has the additional advantage that ice crystals help somewhat, over time, in opening and stretching the fibers.

Finishing

At this point, if we were to throw the skin out on the ground or over a limb, in a few hours it would shrink to a fraction of its size and become quite hard. Our purpose now, therefore, is to prevent this from happening. There are a number of methods of working the skin soft, but I'll cover only the one I currently use, as I find it the easiest. With this method, at any point during the drying process the skin can be rolled (as mentioned above) and placed in the refrigerator or freezer.

The weather does, of course, affect how quickly the skin dries. My personal preference is a slow drying day over a hot, windy one. A fast-drying skin can be hell to keep up with.

What we have to do now is keep the fibers of the skin from doing what they want naturally to do: shrink and pull together as they dry. For this we'll pull and stretch the skin around the lariat all the time that it's drying. I've read one account of a Navaho method of using hands and feet to do the stretching, which I've done successfully on smaller skins in by the fire during the winter. As I've said, various methods work. All methods have one thing in common: to keep every fiber in the skin stretched and open to its fullest while drying. Without the addition of the brain (oils), the rawhide would still dry stiff, though not as stiff as if not stretched. The addition of the oils allows the individual fibers to pull apart and actually swell and soften as they dry, but we must keep each and every fiber stretched to its fullest and moving over and past each other the entire time that the skin's drying. So alternate pulling the skin widthwise and lengthwise. (The above action of the brain isn't scientific fact, just my observations and the easiest way that I know to describe what's taking place.)

Tie one end of the lariat to the base of a tree and the other to a limb about 6' up and pull it tight. Now drape the skin around the rope and pull it in all directions the entire time that it's drying. Begin at the neck and grab a handful of skin and really lay into it. You don't need to worry about the thicker parts of the skin tearing. Lean back and use your entire body weight. Hand over hand, work your way all down the skin to the rump, then turn it halfway and begin pulling the other direction (lengthwise), repeat…and repeat…and repeat.

When pulling the thinner edge areas, such as the flanks, take two handholds, one in about 6" to 8" where the skin's thicker, and pull like hell, and another handhold gripped at the edge with a little lighter pull. This ensures that the heavier central portions get enough stretching and, in the process, you don't overdo and rip through at the thinner edge.

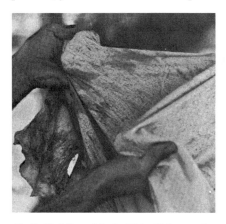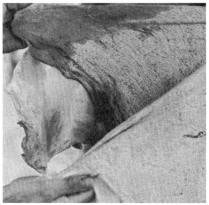

Left: *Holding skin in 6" to 8" from edges and stretching hard.*
Right: *A second grip at the thinner edge and a little lighter pull.*

At any point the skin may be rolled in towels and place in the refrigerator or freezer. As it becomes drier, the towels may be omitted and the remaining moisture allowed to disperse on the skin.

Now here's a major time and effort saver, a tip gleaned from a fellow tanner at the '85 NAPR Western. "Why," says he, "take the extra time and effort to roll the skin in towels and refrigerate? If you've got the time to work it out, just throw it out onto the ground and let it air dry for 10 to 20 minutes. Then stretch it open again…and repeat till dry."

Well, I thought, if that does work—and no reason for it *not* to—I'd better give it a try.

The next skin that I did was an average 10 square footer and I tried it—*and it worked!* And what a time and effort saver it was. It took about 3 1/2 hours for me to finish that skin out, but only half that time was spent stretching. However, you must use caution not to let the skin overdry while it's not being worked, otherwise you'll have to go back to the brain solution. The idea is to allow only a certain amount of the moisture to evaporate (at the same time, the skin will shrink proportionately) and to open up the fibers by stretching before any portion of the skin has dried beyond the point where you're able to easily stretch and soften it. Keep a close watch on it. And if something comes up and you want to quit, wrap and refrigerate or freeze it.

You should also put the remaining brain solution in the fridge before it sits out in a warm room too long, as it will sour in a hurry. You can use it on another skin or you may even have to use it yet again on this one if you haven't gotten complete penetration. I've used the same solution, with the addition of more brain and water, on as many as 10 skins—but that's just being cheap. Fresh solution seems to work better.

At this point I think of the skin as being in one of three stages—wettest, medium wet, and dry. In the wettest stage, the skin will spend more time on the ground than on the rope. The midpoint of drying is the more critical stage, and you'll spend more time stretching or rubbing. When you're pretty sure that the skin is dry and you're just ascertaining that fact, you can spend less time on the rope.

At about the time the thinner areas are drying out, concentrate your efforts on the thicker neck, back, and ham areas.

This is also the stage that the term "blood, sweat, and tears" pertains to. Unconditioned knuckles will blister and bleed. It helps to use bandages over the first knuckle joint, or tight-fitting rubber gloves with fingertips cut off. Time will toughen them.

Begin rubbing the skin around the rope while stretching as soon as it dries enough to do so easily. This helps to crush and stretch the fibers, raises the nap to a fluffier texture, and creates friction that helps speed the drying process somewhat. Rub with vigor.

Don't quit till you're positive that the skin is dry. Any little bit of moisture will detract from a No. 1 quality piece of buckskin. Remember that as long as there's any moisture at all left in the skin, it will shrink and stiffen as it dries. If you stayed with it, the average 10 sq. ft. skin would take approximately 3 1/2 to 4 hours to finish out.

The finished buckskin will be creamy white in color and as soft and fluffy as the best of flannel. But…if this fine piece of material were allowed to get wet (and remember, it will seem to draw moisture, just as brain and other things will draw flies), you'd find yourself back to where you were four hours ago. If it's allowed to dry naturally, it will shrink and stiffen. So though we've got a fine piece of buckskin, we're certainly *not* finished with it. It makes no sense to devise clothing or bags if we can't actually use it.

When stretching, really lay into it.

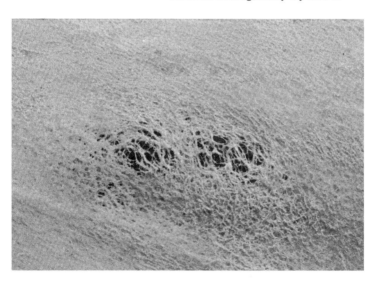

If I were limited to only one photo to illustrate this chapter, this would be it. This shows the detail of the fibers that we're working with.

Smoking

What we do now is smoke the skin. As with the oils of the brain, we need to penetrate smoke into every fiber of the now-soft buckskin. I've heard of various things this does to the skin, but I've never definitively learned how it does it. I do know it works, however, and it's a necessary step to end up with a useful piece of material that will dry soft (or will require only a minimum of rubbing) after a good wetting.

The old way of smoking skins is to sew it into a cone from the neck to the rump, leaving the rump open. Into a hole in the ground (roughly 6" in diameter by 18" deep), place hot coals to a depth of 6" to 8" and cover with punky wood. What's wanted is a smudge of dense, warm smoke. Stake the open end of the skin over the smudge and tie the neck area to a low tree limb or a tripod. Smoke can also be piped to the hanging skin a number of feet away, making it easier to control the fire or smoke and eliminating the possibility of scorching the skin. It's a good idea, also, to sew a piece of material, such as denim or canvas, to the bottom of the skin as additional security against scorching. Keep the skin open so that the warm, dense smoke can penetrate overall. When you see the discoloration of the smoke seeping through the thinner areas, invert the skin and smoke it from the other direction.

This is certainly the quickest way to smoke one skin, or just a few of them. Not including the sewing and setup time, the actual smoking takes from 15 to 30 minutes per side, depending on how dark a shade is desired. This method actually forces the smoke through the skin, whereas in the tipi method (described next) the smoke is absorbed by exposure and therefore takes considerably more time for complete penetration. I seldom use this method, as it requires my constant attention and I normally have a number of skins to smoke at one time. I've read, and been told, that the smoke has to be warm to accomplish its mission. Cold smoke apparently won't work. Myself, I've never tested the cold smoke theory.

I smoke 99 percent of my skins in a tipi. I've used a small shed before, which is fine for pelts or individual skins but too small for any quantity of skins. I know of some people who place their stove right in the lodge. This is inconvenient, to my way of thinking, as they must burn the coals outside and then transport them to the stove to avoid scorching the skins. It's also much easier to tend the smudge in the smokefree out-of-doors. I place my

18' lodge next to a ledge, put the stove below, and pipe the smoke about 12'
to the center of the lodge. I also put a rain cap on the end of the pipe to
help disperse the rising smoke, which promotes more consistent coloring of
the skins.

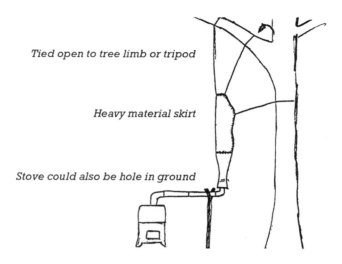

Tied open to tree limb or tripod

Heavy material skirt

Stove could also be hole in ground

Tie the skins to the uppermost part of the poles. I run a piece of heavy
thread through the edge of the skin with a needle and then tie it around the
poles loose enough to hang free so that all parts are exposed to the smoke.
They could also be tacked to the poles. Either very long legs or a stepladder
is necessary. With this method you can hang 8 to 12 skins, depending on the
size of both skins and lodge, and all will come out the same shade and color.
After closing the smoke flaps tight as if for a storm, with liner in place, put
a towel or two in the crotch formed by the poles to slow the escape of the
smoke as much as possible.

Before hanging the skins, build a large fire in the stove, using a
hardwood that will produce long-lasting coals. Oak is my favorite, though
charcoal will suffice. Remember to disconnect the pipe. By the time the
skins are hung and the lodge is closed tight, the coals should be about right.
Replace the pipe so as to heat it quickly to create a good draft, and then
almost immediately cover the coals with fine-shredded, punky wood. The
rottenest, most punky wood that you can find is the best. Don't confuse
soft, wet wood with rotten, punky. If wet when gathered, spread it out to
dry. The wood needs to be punky and unburnable to create the dense smoke
that's necessary.

We don't need to add moisture by burning wet stuff. I've tried using green wood, which burns even hotter than the dry oak. We don't want straight heat, which could scorch the skins. A combination of punky cottonwood and red cedar sawdust leaves my skins a light, bright, lively tan. The same combination used in the first method of forcing the smoke through, is much darker and not nearly so lively. The choice of woods will dictate the final coloring.

I begin this project early in the morning on a day when no rain is expected in the immediate future. Rain will always enter the lodge at the apex and run down the poles, and you're taking a chance when you hang a dozen unsmoked skins in a lodge. A sudden squall would create havoc. By hanging them early in the morning of a clear day, I can begin the actual smoking before 8 a.m. and by the time that I quit for the day at about 10 p.m., I feel secure that if it does rain during the night enough smoke has penetrated the skins that a bit of moisture won't hurt. I would, though, have the skins cut down and in the house at the first hint of a storm within the first day and a half of smoking.

To keep a steady, heavy cloud rising from the stove, you'll have to stir the coals every 20 minutes or so and keep adding more punk when necessary. Every two to three hours you'll also need to rebuild the fire for more coals. *Note:* Don't forget to disconnect the pipe when doing this!

I follow this process for three 12- to 14-hour days while working on other skins only a few feet from the stove. Late in the afternoon of the third day I remove the skins, soak them in cold well water, and hang them from a clothesline. Most everything that I've read on the smoking of skins says to place them in a sack overnight to allow the smoke and color to set. I don't do this and have had no ill effects with my results. After the skins have dried, I pull and rub each one by hand to ensure that the smoke has done its job, and then let them air for a number of days.

That's it. You now have a fine piece of buckskin that's worth $10 or more per square foot. Better than that, you have the satisfaction of having taken a raw piece of material from nature (no kit here!) and, by your own labors, have created a fine, beautiful, useful finished product—something that you can point to and honestly proclaim with pride, *"I made this."*

*Smoke piped to tipi from
stove placed below ledge.*

*A number of skins
hanging in tipi for smoking.*

"Hair-on" Supplement

Leaving the hair on when brain tanning requires the application of a few different rules. The skin (pelt, hide, whatever) should *not* be soaked in the brain solution as with buckskin, as this can result in hair slippage. Instead, the brain should be painted on the former flesh side, allowed to dry, *the dried brain "film" scraped off,* and then repeated till you're certain that you have *complete* penetration. Remember that you're penetrating from only one side. With the same thickness buckskin, that might require eight applications (soakings and wringings), but here you'll have to do more than twice that number. Thinner pelts (fox, cats) might get by with only one or two applications (I would do four or five at least; remember that you can't possibly overbrain). The thickest, toughest *pelt* that I've done is the beaver. After successfully doing five extra-large, blanket-sized ones, I wouldn't hesitate to apply the solution as many as 40 to 50 times. This means lots of work, though the fine finished results have been well worth the effort. (I can do a couple of buckskins in the time that it takes to do a large beaver.) The beaver I skin "open" and stretch around on a willow hoop or some such. I lace it, using needle and artificial sinew (waxed nylon) thread, stitches about 1" apart. Lace it with the holes pretty close to the edge and be especially careful around the face. What we're trying to do is save all we can.

I prefer to work all other pelts "case" skinned. The dried pelt can be kept on the stretcher for the brainings. When the legs are left on, I staple them open to thin slats. I skin the paws as open as I can and soak them in the brain (they should be "tanned," but I know nothing of that; I only do things the natural way, though soaking in the oils of the brain can't hurt). Ears should be skinned out to the very tip; I also soak these. All meats and fats must be removed from these areas or they will eventually rot, if gotten wet, and the hair will then slip. The final coat of brain can be applied, applied, and applied once more. Saturate it as much as you can, then maybe place a warm, damp towel (damp with brain solution is fine) on the flesh side, place it in a plastic sack, and allow it to stand till it becomes as pliable as when green. Don't overdo it, or it could begin to rot and cause hair slippage. Then work it over the rope or by hand till it's dry and soft.

For deer with the hair on, I wouldn't even bother with brain tanning, The hollow hairs of the deer break off if you even look hard at them. The only practical use for a hair-on deer is as a wall hanging, and even then it doesn't need to be soft. I have done one deer robe. No more! It was nice, but you can't do anything with it but pick up hairs wherever you might visit, eventually ending up with a piece of buckskin anyhow. It's just not worth the extra work, *and it* is *a huge amount of extra work.* I've read where Indians just threw the raw skin on the floor of the lodge, and when the hair all fell out they had a softened piece of rawhide ready to brain into buckskin. One that you wanted for a wall hanging could be saturated with pure neat's-foot oil (for better penetration), or brained and only worked semisoft.

Yet if you insist—and also for elk, buffalo, and other creatures—here are some tips to kinda help you along.

Follow the preparation steps up through page 288. Now, I'm not talking about skins or hides with the legs or faces left on. Then begin to paint the brain solution on, scraping between coatings as with the pelts. Apply, apply, and apply again—you can't do too much. *You* will have to judge as to how many coatings each pelt will need. Finally, lay the frame out flat and apply the brain till the skin's saturated. (You might even repeat this several times.) When the pelt's as pliable as when green, *don't* cut it from the frame, as there will be too much bulk for you to work over a rope. Instead, stand the frame up and, beginning with a canoe paddle (or something similar), begin to run a tool down the hide. You'll be stretching the hide and at the same time squeegeeing the moisture out. You'll only be working the flesh side. The epidermis will restrict the stretching process, and you'll work your butt off, but keep at it. You *must,* till it's dry and soft. As the hide gets drier, graduate to a smaller stick to stretch with (a rounded-down ax handle will work well).

Along about now you'll begin to wish that you hadn't begun this project. You'll think it's a "buster," but it'll be worth it. Someone once showed me an old photo of Native American women "playing" by bouncing children up and down on a buffalo hide like a trampoline. "Playing," hell—they were stretching the hide soft! Whichever way you decide to do this, it must be continued till it's completely finished. No half-hour breaks here. For this project it would be best to have one or more helpers. If you've properly prepared the surface and applied enough brain to achieve *complete* penetration, *and* if you keep the proper stretching up till it's completely dry, you'll end up with a fine robe indeed.

It's best to smoke the finished pelt or robe in a smokehouse or in the tipi. If the legs and face are left on, it'll be impossible to sew into a bag.

This is only a quickie jotting of supplementary notes for hair-on brain tanning and is far from complete. Still, when used in conjunction with the rest of this book, the above material should help you to end up with a fine product.

Sewing with Sinew

Assuming that you're reading this because you're either involved in buckskinning or just interested in a more natural way of life, I want to show you how to use another completely natural product for the threads when turning your buckskin into clothing or whatever other products you're making.

Sinew, on a critter, is a tendon. "Critter," in our case, is most likely a deer. On our critter we have two sources of convenient, usable sinew: the tendons of the legs and the loin sinew, of which there are two flat strips, one lying on either side of the backbone on top of the meat.

The leg tendons are shorter and more difficult to work into threads. Since I have no first-hand experience working with leg tendons, I'll cover only the more easily workable loin sinew.

Elk loin sinew will run a little over 2' in length, buffalo closer to 3'. Deer sinew, which I mostly use, runs about 15" to 18" long and is finer than the other two animals'. Sinew can be obtained from some buckskinning supply houses. A single strip contains a hearty supply of threads.

I obtain all my deer sinew directly from the critter. Stripping isn't a difficult chore, but when deer are usually available to me the temperature has a tendency to be well below the freezing mark. Although working with bare hands makes the job of removal much easier, it can be mighty uncomfortable. The sinew can't be removed from a frozen carcass.

A dull knife run under tendon while attached to deer.

Final scraping clean of strip. Bottom has been pulled loose from carcass while top remains attached.

Most times, the sinew is available from a deer whose skin is also obtainable. After skinning, make a cut up against and parallel to the backbone about 1/4" deep. With your fingers, pull away the outer layer of fat and expose the silvery sinew lying atop the meat and running from the shoulder to the hip, 1" to 2" wide and tapering. Take a dull knife (a butter knife works well) and about midway in length run this under the sinew and begin working the blade in either direction, separating the meat from the sinew. **Caution:** *Too sharp a blade will cut the tendon.* Clean the strip only to where it enters the hip, or goes into the shoulder, whichever way you're working. Leave it attached to the carcass and clean it the other way. When it's separated the entire length, but still attached at both ends, continue to run the knife back and forth several times to get the strip as clean as possible. Remove all meat and fat. When this is as clean as you can get it, begin to work the knife into the hip till it pulls free at that end and then remove it from the shoulder. You'll need to cut somewhat into the meat at the ends to free the entire strip. Once it's loose from the critter, again scrape both sides till completely clean and then lay it out on a flat surface to dry. When you buy loin sinew from a source, this is what you'll get.

The dried loin sinew strip.

Getting individual threads from this is easy. Grab the strip between thumb and forefinger of each hand, close together, and work the sinew back and forth and around and around for a few seconds. This will break the strip into individual threads. Do this the entire length and you'll have a real conglomeration of threads that can be stripped off as needed in the thickness desired: thicker threads for sewing soles to moccasins, medium threads for general-purpose garment and bag sewing, and fine delicate threads necessary for quill or bead work. These finer strands are the most difficult to work loose in any length, but with a bit of care and patience it can be done.

Sinew is surprisingly strong, as it must be to have served as bowstrings for the very powerful Plains Indians' sinew-backed bow. It's certainly as strong as most of our modern-day threads.

Sinew threads can be pulled off individually as needed, or many made up in advance. When making them ahead of time I find it easier to separate them if the strip is wetted first (after having broken the threads apart).

Toward the middle of the strip, at the edge, begin to work the fibers free in the thickness desired. As this is worked loose you'll find that toward the wide end of the strip the thread will be somewhat thicker than at the other. This is the forward end of the thread. When the thread is separated wet, I use my mouth on it till soft, then lay it on a flat surface to dry. When you're ready to begin sewing, wet the thread thoroughly as before and thread the thick end through a needle (a glovers needle works best) and go to it. Before the availability of the needle, the Indians would let the thicker end dry, and that would stiffen enough to suffice as a needle through a hole punched with an awl. You'll discover that with brain-tanned skins you won't require a thimble.

Instead of a knot at the end of the thread, sew through the material once and then again to create a loop through which you'll wrap (tie) the thread three times and then pull tight. Let about 3/4" of the tail of the thread lie in line with your stitching and sew it under as you go. As the sinew dries it will shrink slightly and stiffen, conforming to the stitching and creating a tight knot and seam. Pull the stitches as tight as possible. When the thread breaks you'll know that it's too tight. When you reach the end of one thread, tie it off as you began (a loop and wrapped three times). Pull it tight, and let the end of the thread run in line with and under the next stitches.

Breaking threads loose by twisting in fingers.

Entire strip broken (took about three minutes).

When the end of the seam is reached, tie the thread off twice, just in case. Then take the needle and run the thread "through" the center of the buckskin for about 1" and cut it off (try this with commercially tanned leather!—can't be done). Take the rounded butt end of your scissors, or something similar, and flatten the seams. Of course, all seams are sewn inside out. As mentioned before, all sewing with brain tan is on the former flesh side, the former hair side being the outside.

Separated threads ready for use.

When finished, the seams will hardly be visible, the knots will be almost indistinguishable, and no loose threads will be hanging.

By using sinew, you'll be just one more notch up on today's technological world. You'll have taken another small step toward self-fulfillment and sufficiency. And you'll enjoy knowing that an otherwise fine piece of workmanship in your finished product has gained a bit more value with just the slightest bit of extra effort.

Smoked skins hanging from line.

Index

processing, 182–200
skinning, 188–90, 281–82
Deerskin pots and buckets, 214–15,
217, 219–20
Digging sticks as tools, 59–60
Drills for firemaking, 2–22, 68

Entrance of shelters, 80

Field dressing, 182–87
Firemaking, primitive, 1–34
bow drills, 2–17
cordage, 23–33
hand drills, 2, 17–22, 68
tips, 33–34
Firing methods in pottery making,
263–69
Fish, trapping, 167–69
Fletching in arrow construction,
138–42
Flintknapping, 36–53
rules, 41–42
safety concerns, 38, 51
techniques, 40, 42–52
Floor of shelters, 78
Food preparation, 201–20
tools, 73–74

Gathering, 170–72
Glue
in arrow construction, 142
in bow construction, 123–28

Hafting, 63–65
Hand drills for firemaking, 2, 17–22,
68
parts, 18
using, 19–22
Hantavirus, 146–50
Hot rock cooking, 213–19

Insects, 176

Jerky, 177–80

Kilns in pottery making, 269, 270

Lean-tos, 83–86

Mano and metate, 73
Meat
cutting, 196–200
hanging, 181–82
and hunting/trapping, 145–69
nutritional value, 151, 177
preservation, 176–80
See also Deer
Mortar and pestle, 74
Mud pack, cooking in, 204–205

Nets, 165–66, 168
Nuts, gathering, 171

Packrats, 171–72
trapping, 163
Paddling in pottery making, 255
Paiute deadfall trigger system, 158–60
Parfletche, 239
Pemmican, 177, 179
Pottery, primitive, 247–72
aboriginal, 271
clay, 248–52
construction, 255–62
firing methods, 263–69
materials, 248–54
safety concerns, 255–56
temper, 252–54

Rabbit sticks, 170
Rocks. *See* Stones
Roof of shelters, 78–79

Sandstone as tool, 55
Seeds, gathering, 171
Shells as tools, 53–54
Shelters, primitive, 75–100
design, 78–80
generic construction, 92–100
lean-tos, 83–86
location, 77
materials, 80–81
safety concerns, 77
thatched wickiups, 86–91
wickiups, 81–82, 86–91

Sinews
  and bow staves, 121–29
  sewing, 307–11
Skinning, 188–90, 281–82
Skins for brain tanning, 281–82
Smoke hole of shelters, 79
Snakes, 171
Snares and trap lines, 151–69
Spear-throwers, 172–75
Staves
  curing, 107–108
  heating and bending, 113–15
  locating, 107
  and sinew glueing, 121–29
  stringing, 117–19
Sticks
  as tools, 59–60
  throwing, 170
Stones, 56
  containers, 237–38
  cooking, 213–19
  as tools, 56, 61–65, 73–74

Tanning. *See* Brain tanning
Temper in pottery making, 252–54
Thatched wickiups, 86–91
Throwing sticks. *See also* Atlatls
Tools, primitive, 35–74
  adzes, 66
  antlers, 56, 57–59
  awls, 60–61
  blunt instruments, 55–56

bones, 56–57
bow and arrow construction, 106, 132
celt, 61–65
digging sticks, 59–60
flintknapping, 36–53
food preparation, 73–74
hafting, 63–65
shells, 53–54
sticks, 59–60
stones, 56, 61–65, 73–74
vises, 67
wood, 55
working with, 68–73
Trap lines and snares, 145, 151–69
Trapping
  birds, 165–66
  fish, 167–69
  packrats, 163
  See also Trap lines and snares
Trigger systems for traps, 152–63
Twining in basket making, 224

Vises as tools, 67

Walls of shelters, 78
Wickiups, 81–82, 86–91
Wood
  containers, 73, 243–45
  as tools, 55
  See also specific wooden items
Wooden awls as tools, 60–61

Resources

Primitive living and survival is an abstract subject. Except for a very few people (such as members of the military involved in evasion or escape), no one will ever need these skills. The most primitive of cultures absorb modern skills as quickly as they are exposed to them (use of steel, firearms, and so on), and all cultures have been exposed. If we were to be teaching survival skills in a modern, realistic manner to the general public, we would write material to reflect this.

We are primitive by choice, and our materials (including this book) teach you how to successfully live with nothing. If you are looking for "real-world" information or trying to stay alive when the chips fall, you will want to check out two books by Cody Lundin: *98.6 Degrees: The Art of Keeping Your Ass Alive* (Layton, Utah: Gibbs Smith, 2003) and *When All Hell Breaks Loose: Stuff You Need to Survive When Disaster Strikes* (Gibbs Smith, 2007).

You also may visit the authors' website, www.prairiewolf.net, where you can order their books:

Primitive Wilderness Skills, Applied and Advanced
"How-to" Build This Log Cabin for $3,000

Instructional DVDs and videotapes are also available, showing the principles and techniques covered in this book. Subjects include primitive fire and cordage, bow and arrow, deer from field to freezer, brain-tan buckskin, breaking rock and making arrowheads, constructing shelters, and creating bows.

About the Authors

John and Geri McPherson have gathered wilderness skills, to some extent, for their entire lives, John growing up in the Appalachian Mountains of New York State and Geri in the woods of Minnesota. They continue to live on the homestead that they have built (log home and outbuildings, outhouse, no electricity, gravity-fed water), beginning in 1978. Their focus has been the primitive side of outdoor and wilderness skills, and since the mid-1980s they have been writing about and teaching what is presented in this book. "Survivorman" Les Stroud trained with them on two occasions during the early 1990s.

They have been featured in many local, national, and international media over the years, including Outdoor Life, Sports Afield, Backwoods Home Magazine, The History Channel, National Public Radio, and Voice of America TV. Their writings have appeared in other media, as well. Known internationally as leaders in the field of primitive skills, John (eight years a paratrooper) and Geri McPherson are in their fourth year of teaching these skills to the survival instructors of the U.S. Army Special Operations Survival, Evasion, Resistance, and Escape (SERE) school.